T0323863

Luxury and Fashion Marketing

The globalization of the world's markets has forced luxury brands to, in turn, become global and accessible in many developing countries and emerging markets. As a result, the demand for these luxury products has increased globally, creating a need for an education in luxury that acknowledges the global perspective yet, at the same time, incorporates subtle regional nuances into luxury and fashion marketing.

Keeping this global and regional perspective, *Luxury and Fashion Marketing: The Global Perspective* examines the elements of luxury marketing that contribute to superior luxury brand performance. Specifically, this volume focuses on mission statements, logos, airport retailing, franchising, challenges in luxury marketing, fashion relating to politics, environment, and beachwear, and case studies on luxury brands and emerging markets.

Luxury and Fashion Marketing: The Global Perspective is unique in that it is written in a simple and engaging style to explain the theories and concepts of luxury in relation to the ordinary in the global context. Each chapter has to-do activities, making the book essential reading for students, trainers, and practitioners interested in luxury and fashion marketing and management.

Dr. Satyendra Singh is an international business consultant and Professor of Marketing and International Business at the University of Winnipeg, Canada.

Routledge Studies in Marketing

This series welcomes proposals for original research projects that are either single or multi-authored or an edited collection from both established and emerging scholars working on any aspect of marketing theory and practice and provides an outlet for studies dealing with elements of marketing theory, thought, pedagogy and practice.

It aims to reflect the evolving role of marketing and bring together the most innovative work across all aspects of the marketing 'mix'—from product development, consumer behaviour, marketing analysis, branding, and customer relationships, to sustainability, ethics and the new opportunities and challenges presented by digital and online marketing.

Understanding the Higher Education Market in Africa
Edited by Emmanuel Mogaji, Felix Maringe, and Robert Ebo Hinson

Internal Marketing
Theories, Perspectives, and Stakeholders
David M. Brown

Stakeholder Involvement in Social Marketing
Challenges and Approaches to Engagement
Edited by Kathy Knox, Krzysztof Kubacki, and Sharyn Rundle-Thiele

Decoding Coca-Cola
A Biography of a Global Brand
Edited by Robert Crawford, Linda Brennan, and Susie Khamis

Driving Consumer Engagement in Social Media
Influencing Electronic Word of Mouth
Anna Bianchi

For more information about this series, please visit: www.routledge.com/Routledge-Studies-in-Marketing/book-series/RMKT

Luxury and Fashion Marketing
Marketing

The Global Perspective

Satyendra Singh

Routledge
Taylor & Francis Group

NEW YORK AND LONDON

First published 2021
by Routledge
52 Vanderbilt Avenue, New York, NY 10017

and by Routledge
2 Park Square, Milton Park, Abingdon, Oxon, OX14 4RN

Routledge is an imprint of the Taylor & Francis Group, an informa business

© 2021 Taylor & Francis

Library of Congress Cataloging-in-Publication Data
Names: Singh, Satyendra, 1966– author.
Title: Luxury and fashion marketing : the global perspective /
    Satyendra Singh.
Description: New York, NY : Routledge, 2021. | Series: Routledge
    studies in marketing | Includes bibliographical references and index.
Identifiers: LCCN 2020031129 (print) | LCCN 2020031130 (ebook) |
    ISBN 9781138576438 (hbk) | ISBN 9781351269605 (ebk)
Subjects: LCSH: Fashion merchandising. | Luxuries—Marketing.
    Branding (Marketing)
Classification: LCC HD9940.A2 S58 2021 (print) | LCC HD9940.
    A2 (ebook) | DDC 658.8—dc23
LC record available at https://lccn.loc.gov/2020031129
LC ebook record available at https://lccn.loc.gov/2020031130

ISBN: 978-1-138-57643-8 (hbk)
ISBN: 978-0-367-65083-4 (pbk)
ISBN: 978-1-351-26960-5 (ebk)

Typeset in Sabon
by Apex CoVantage, LLC

Contents

Acknowledgments

This research-based book is the result of many years of teaching, traveling, and conducting research in the areas of luxury and fashion marketing. My thanks are due to the store managers, sales assistants, airport retailers, and handicraft artists in many countries who offered me their insights from a global perspective. I am also grateful to the following professors and professionals for their support for the book:

Mr. Ernest Amponsah, Regent University, Accra, Ghana
Professor Tapas Ranjan Dash, CamEd Business School, Phnom Penh, Cambodia
Professor Hugh Grant, University of Winnipeg, Winnipeg, Canada
Professor Rosalie Harms, University of Winnipeg, Winnipeg, Canada
Professor Meera Kaur, University of Manitoba, Winnipeg, Canada
Professor Peter Lewa, United States International University Africa (USIU-A), Nairobi, Kenya
Professor Michael Pasco, De La Salle University, Manila, Philippines
Mr. Ravi Prakash, Descher Garments Pvt Ltd, Windhoek, Namibia
Professor Irina Vashko, Academy of Public and Business Administration, Minsk, Belarus

I sincerely thank the two anonymous reviewers for reviewing the book proposal and providing me with their valuable feedback. Their comments have been immensely useful in improving the book and its logic. It was my good fortune to meet Editor David Varley, who saw the value in the book proposal and encouraged me to see it in print. Thank you for accepting the book proposal. It was also my pleasure to work with incoming Editor Brianna Ascher and Naomi Round Cahalin, editorial assistant for processing the book; thank you.

Dr. Satyendra Singh
Professor, Marketing and International Business
University of Winnipeg, Canada

About the Author

Dr. Satyendra Singh is Professor of Marketing and International Business, Faculty of Business and Economics, University of Winnipeg, Canada, and editor-in-chief of the *Journal of the Academy of Business and Emerging Markets* (JABEM), Canada. Dr. Singh's research interests lie in developing countries and emerging markets, with particular emphasis on Africa and Asia on issues relating to the impact of transitional governments' economic policies on business performance. Dr. Singh has published widely in reputed international journals such as IMR, TIBR, IMI, SIJ, MIP, JSM, JGM, and MD, among others, and presented papers at international conferences such as AIB, AM, AMA, AMS, ASAC, BAM, EMAC, and WMC, to list a few. Currently, Dr. Singh chairs the Academy of Business and Emerging Markets (ABEM) Conference, www.abem.ca/conference. Dr. Singh is a frequent keynote speaker and has traveled to more than 90 countries to teach, train, or consult.

1 Introduction

Aim and Scope of the Book

The aim of the book is to provide thought-provoking contemporary concepts relating to luxury and fashion marketing in the global context. These concepts answer many intriguing questions relating to luxury and fashion. For example, should mission statements for luxury brands be different from non-luxury brands? Do luxury products need to be the same (or different) in different cultures? Why is it difficult to sell luxury products in some countries? Can luxury beachwear be positioned to target non-swimmers? Do luxury brands really need logos? Indeed, the book aims to generate debate and test the new concepts. In short, this book provides new concepts, balanced arguments, short cases on luxury brands and emerging luxury markets, and experiential learning exercises.

Who Is the Book For?

The book is suitable for upper-level undergraduate and graduate business students with interests in luxury and fashion marketing. The book introduces the topics and concepts and then moves on to the analytical level through the use of theory, examples, and applications. Application of the concepts is achieved through the *experiential learning exercises*. Practitioners will find the exercises equally beneficial. Graduate students can turn the theoretical concepts into testable hypotheses.

How Is the Book Different?

This is a comprehensive research-based book. It includes luxury marketing, fashion marketing, cases on emerging luxury markets, and luxury brands—all in one. The book is different from other books about luxury marketing in that the chapters are innovative, relevant, and analytical in nature. In some cases, the topics in the chapters can be iconoclastic in nature and highly debatable. The idea is to avoid repetition of what is obvious about luxury and advance the luxury field by proposing new topics and concepts—for example, role of mission statements in luxury, power of logos in conveying messages and how they are developed, fashion as a political statement, and counterfeit luxury product life cycle, among others. The book has interest-ing contents and new applications in the context of luxury in the global environment. Further, the chapters are written parsimoniously and thus are kept short. Focus is on concept implementation through the *experiential learning exercises* presented at the end of many chapters.

Organization of the Book

The book is organized into *four* parts (luxury marketing, fashion marketing, cases on emerging luxury markets, and cases on luxury brands). Part I has *five* chapters relating to luxury marketing, whereas Part II has *two* chapters covering fashion marketing. Part III consists of short cases on *four* emerging luxury markets—Colombia, Indonesia, Vietnam, and South Africa. Finally, Part IV contains *four* short case studies on luxury brands—Apple, BMW, Burberry, and Gucci.

Part I (Luxury Marketing)

Mission statements reflect a firm's objectives and values and serve as a guiding principle. *Chapter 2* explores characteristics of both mission statements—luxury and ordinary brands—with respect to the role of emo-tion, innovation, communications, and strategic management in creating a superior business performance.

Effective logos can also lead to superior business performance. Logos are a visual *word* and convey a distinct message to customers. But logo devel-opment remains a mystery, as a logo can be of any shape, size, and color, among other features. *Chapter 3* demystifies logo development by examin-ing the logic of having such shapes and sizes, and their impact on drawing the attention of customers. Arguments are also made for having *no logo* but yet be recognizable.

The increase in air travel and construction of new airports worldwide provide unique opportunity for luxury brands to market their products at airports. Nearly half of airports' income comes from non-aeronautical activities. *Chapter 4* discusses the unique airport retail environment for the marketing of luxury products and services, explains the impulsive and apathetic behavior of travelers, and highlights the franchising strategy and other luxury retail options and outlets.

One retail option is to make use of Internet technology. The technology has forced marketing managers to move away from traditional marketing tools and adopt the new evolving, more expressive electronic marketing tools. In this context, *Chapter 5* focuses on the five aspects—virtual reality, online marketing, social media, mobile marketing, and celebrity endorsements—of contemporary marketing. Use of semiotic communications in marketing is also discussed.

Luxury brands are inherently in conflict with marketing or publicity ini-tiatives. Initiatives need to balance brands' exclusivity by having limited public exposure against the visibility required by any publicity. Striking the balance is challenging. *Chapter 6* highlights four such areas of challenges relating to luxury marketing, publicity, and public relations: charitable activities, counterfeit products, corporate social responsibility, and government advertisement regulations.

Part II (Fashion Marketing)

The fashion industry is one of the most prominent industries in both advanced countries and emerging markets. It is characterized by its fast-growing trends and various kinds of styles. Fashion attracts everybody, but it takes confidence to articulate personal style and preference and make a statement. Keeping this viewpoint, *Chapter 7* explores three topics relating to fashion: political fashion, eco fashion, and ethnic fashion. Luxury beachwear and underwear marketing is also discussed in light of changing consumer preferences.

With the rise in disposable income and changing preferences in emerging markets, *Chapter 8* identifies the influence of five factors—the Indian consumer, Indian apparel and fashion, economy, culture, and media and films—on the decision-making process for fashion products in India. This chapter also discusses marketing strategy.

Part III (Cases on Emerging Luxury Markets)

Chapters 9, 10, 11, and *12* relate to Colombia, Indonesia, Vietnam, and South Africa, respectively. These are short yet insightful cases in discussing issues relating to marketing of luxury and fashion products in these countries.

Part IV (Cases on Luxury Brands)

Chapters 13, 14, 15, and *16* relate to Apple, BMW, Burberry, and Gucci, respectively. The mini cases are selected carefully so that the concepts discussed in the book can be applied to them, in hopes of identifying possible remedies for the situations presented in the cases.

Chapter 17 concludes the book.

Part I
Luxury Marketing

2 Mission Statements

Introduction

Mission statements are written to portray organizational objectives and values consistent with those of the key shareholders (Peyrefitte & David 2006). Comparison of mission statements exists in multiple studies. Zandstra (2012) explores the differences and similarities in mission statements of Christian elementary schools in the United States and the Netherlands. Comparisons across industries are also common. Mission statements have been used to define a zoo's role and understand the relationship between conservation and education (Patrick, Matthews, Ayers, & Tunnicliffe 2007). Different types of businesses in the same industry can also be a basis for mission statement analysis such as the comparison of for-profit and not-for-profit hospitals in the United States (Bolon 2005). A comparison of religious colleges and universities also reveals stylistic differences among different institutions with regard to vision, complexity, optimism, and even the establishment's use of language in an effort to unify the campus (Abelman & Dalessandro 2009). Mo-Ching Yeung (2013) analyzed the content of mission statements of business schools to explore the application of system thinking and quality management concept, whereas Firmin and Gilson (2009) analyzed the contents of the Council of Christian Colleges and Universities to discover the degree to which they included religion in their mission statements.

In this chapter, we focus on the topic of mission statements of luxury and ordinary products and services. The categorization of a certain topic does not necessarily mean that their mission or vision is much different than another category (Bolon 2005). Because marketing of luxury brands is different from ordinary brands, conveying an image of quality, authenticity, and lifestyle, while amplifying the essence of a product into a physical and interactive experience, has become important in positively influencing the purchasing process (Atwal & Williams 2009). In this regard, a mission statement is the image of a company's character that embodies a company's soul (Ireland & Hitt 1992). Thus, a mission statement can be considered a form of marketing tool for a brand that forms its image. It is the uniqueness in marketing approaches through mission statements that leads to designing different mission statements for different products such as luxury versus ordinary. In fact, several topics relating to luxury brands have been studied—for example, the concept of luxury brand loyalty and sustainability (Younghee, Won-Moo, & Minsung 2012) and brand exclusivity (Cailleux, Mignot, & Kapferer 2009), among others. In this chapter, we explain components of mission statements, characteristics of luxury brand mission statements, emotion and innovation in luxury brand mission statements, arguments for *no mission statements*, ordinary brand mission statements, communications, strategic management, and business performance.

Components of Mission Statements

Pearce and David (1987) identify the nine essential components in an effective mission statement: philosophy, customers, products and services, target markets, technology, growth, employees, self-concept, and public image. Other scholars have also detected the presence of these components in mission statements. The study by Bartkus, Glassman, and McAfee (2004) compared the content of mission statements of European, Japanese, and US firms in varying institutional structures and found that firms used at least half the recommended components in their mission statements. Another comparative study of comparison between mission statements of Chinese and US firms indicated differences in cultural structure but similarities in content (Angriawan, Barczyk, Firlej, Rarick, & Nickerson 2010). Yet another study based on academic institutions found differences in mission statements only with regard to organizational longevity and social responsibility (Smith, Heady, Carson, & Carson 2001). Based on the findings and the fact that luxury brand status in the marketplace may influence the way firms communicate through their mission statements, we may expect some differences in the contents of mission statements between luxury and ordinary brands.

Characteristics of Luxury Brand Mission Statements

Characteristics of luxury brands include high price, excellent quality, specialized distribution channels, prestige image associated with the brand, an element of uniqueness or exclusivity, and a history of high performance (Beverland & Luxton 2005). Luxury brands also fall under the rarity principle, which states that the prestige of a brand can become eroded if too many people own it (Dubois & Paternault 1995). Social status is also associated with luxury brands. However, unlike ordinary mission statements, luxury brands appear to use creativity and innovation in their mission statements that contribute to building a unique corporate identity and engaging niche target audiences. Luxury brands missions focus on creating a unique customer experience, the internal company culture, and the values that guide daily decisions and business practices. Thus, each mission statement is unique, as it is tailored exclusively for luxury products and services. For example, the Louis Vuitton statement relates to the most refined qualities of Western "Art de Vivre" (art of living) around the world, is synonymous with both elegance and creativity, blends tradition and innovation, and kindles dreams and fantasy. Consumers who are motivated to buy luxury products go beyond specifications and features of products. They are driven by values also. Porsche's values in its mission statement are excellent. Porsche is committed to providing impeccable service to its demanding clientele of premium cars, engaging in the utmost possible customer attention and care in all aspects of the business, and creating a connection in the workplace with shared passion for its vision and goals. Thus, luxury brands differentiate themselves from traditional brands based on their core values and characteristics such as exclusivity, craftsmanship, and aesthetic attribute. The Montblanc mission statement even stirs its customers' emotions. It states that the Montblanc pen is not just a pen; it is a fine writing instrument designed to be collected and cherished. It is far from ordinary or even premium. It is only for those who truly value its unique and innate quality.

Emotion

Luxury brands target audiences with more pleasurable psychologically arousing feelings towards their core mission and values, whereas ordinary brand mission statements predominantly emphasize the physical features and characteristics of their products and services. Luxury brands are aware that personal feelings and experiences shape consumers' evaluations of brands, so they communicate their brand identity through emotionally appealing statements. Emotional branding creates strong emotional attachments between consumers and the brand (Kim & Sullivan 2019). Emotion-evocative luxury brand mission statements lead to a favorable brand awareness, reputation, and loyalty, as luxury products fulfill two main functions: gaining acceptance from others and rewarding ourselves for an accomplishment (Page 2020). Therefore, the decision-making process of purchasing luxury products shifts from rationally objective reasons to emotionally evocative and subjective motives, with the need for mission statements to validate the emotional coding scheme (Straker & Wrigley 2018). The Audi mission statement appears to be emotional. It reads: "Our success has been achieved through creativity, commitment, and the ability to generate enthusiasm. The wishes and emotions of our customers are the guiding principles behind our every action." Usually, luxury brand mission statements incorporate words such as "uniqueness," "happiness," "excitement," "creativity," "enthusiasm," "emotions," "positivity," and "encouragement" to stimulate positive emotions in customers. So, luxury mission statements appear to be more emotion-based than logic-driven (Farfan 2018). Some luxury brands have also used the concept of emotion in their mission statements to fill the gap between current self and potential self of their target audience. For example, the premium Biotherm beauty boutique helps women view their bodies as a source of attractiveness and confidence (not anxiety) by stating in their mission: "fostering their self-esteem and full potential." The goal of such luxury mission brand statements is to outline how their products will contribute to positive transformation for their consumers, who have felt powerless to change their lives themselves (Kim & Sullivan 2019). Indeed, it is not only a high price tag that may make a product luxurious, but rather it is also the emotional connection that comes from using the product that can affect the degree of its luxury more than its economic value.

Innovation

Luxury brands are innovative and adaptive to the audience. Innovation is the process of creating a new product or improving it to meet the needs of a target audience. Apple has an extraordinary mission statement based on the concept of innovation which directs its employees to develop the next generation of products to be thinner, lighter, and better, while signaling to its customers to expect the same. In another luxury example of innovation, the iconic Italian high-fashion brand Brioni focuses on innovation and individualization of products. This brand is so unique in its innovation, design, and comfort that it includes prestigious customers such as US President Donald J. Trump. Innovative mission statements have also been found to be effective in targeting audience in emerging markets such as China, whose new class of wealthy customers is willing to purchase luxury brands with outstanding quality (Schade, Hegner, Horstmann, & Brinkmann 2016). Sales of luxury brands in emerging markets have shown significant consistent growth, where customers seek to acquire recognizable luxury brands and use them as a way to demonstrate their success to others. True, different people perceive luxury differently. In the emerging markets of India, the fashion and lifestyle magazine *Vogue India* shows the innovation of Indian fashion designers and jewelers who specialize in bridal wear and jewelry. Innovation has also played a significant role in sustainability issues such as *eco fashion* relating to luxury products and fashion. Eco fashion is part of a growing philosophy of design, production, and consumption, and protection of the environment. The trend includes the innovative behavior of a growing number of firms and segments of fashionable consumers (Woodside & Fine 2019). Bamboo-based shirts and bikes are examples of luxury brands' endeavors to be innovative while protecting the environment. It is also true that some luxury brands are not fully able to commit to protecting or maintaining environmental standards.

Arguments for No Mission Statements

Opponents argue that firms without written mission statements may perform equally well because (1) the costs of developing a mission statement may not be economical (David 1989), (2) companies lack the skills to develop customer services mentioned in mission statements (Wright 2002), (3) mission statements do not deliver anticipated results (David 1989), and

(4) few people read them (Ireland & Hitt 1992). Some luxury brands do not have mission statements as such but are known for their quality and high standards worldwide. The luxury brand Rolex—established in 1905 in the UK as a leading global brand in the watchmaking industry—does not appear to have a formal mission statement. It can be argued that development of a mission statement is an outdated approach to strategic management and communicating an organization's vision. This view may be supported by the ever-changing needs of the global consumer and the different strategies needed to maintain customer orientation and competitive advantage in the ever-evolving global marketplace. Perhaps mission statements cannot reflect these changes so quickly. However, most brands, luxury or ordinary, have mission and vision statements and strategies associated with them.

Ordinary Brand Mission Statements

Ordinary brands can be defined as brands that are attainable by the masses. These brands usually have a relatively low price and offer low-to-medium quality and services. Typically, ordinary brand mission statements often emphasize the physical attributes and benefits derived from buying the products or services that motivate consumers to maximize the utilities or satisfaction from the purchases. For example, the Old Navy mission is about making current American fashion essentials accessible to every family; H&M's mission is to drive long-lasting positive change and improve living conditions by investing in people, communities, and innovative ideas. Similarly, Ford strives to make people's lives better by making mobility accessible and affordable. And Claire's is the world's leading brand for fun, affordable, and fashionable jewelry, accessories, and beauty products. It embraces every girl's individuality and love of style by providing her a platform for personal discovery and self-expression. Claire's mission appears similar to the luxury Biotherm skincare firm, whose mission is that every urban man and woman can possess flawless skin and ignite their inner potential to face everyday challenges. Although there may be some similarities in the content of mission statements between ordinary and luxury brands, the way the missions are achieved and communicated are indeed different (e.g. high price, high quality, and messages associated with luxury brands, among others) in both categories.

Communications

Mission statements can influence organizations and their employees (Collins & Porras 1996). The statements let the employees know the mission and values of the company as a whole, and how they should be presented to the public. Mission statements may act as outlines and communications tools for use by top managers to direct and focus their own planning and that of their subordinates, because a mission statement is the inspiring words chosen by a company to clearly convey the direction of the organization

(Klemm, Sanderson & Luffman 1991). Mission statements can set and manage customers' expectations. For example, the mission statement of the premier American Airlines Customer Service Plan states that they are in business to provide safe, dependable, and friendly air transportation to their customers, in the hopes that they will fly with the airline again and again, whereas the mission of a regular brand, such as Spirit Airlines, is to provide a safe, market-responsive, customer-oriented air transportation product; a high level of customer service; and efficient, friendly, and prompt service. So it appears that in both cases the companies' philosophies communicated through their mission statements do not vary greatly, as both statements include similar, although not identical, visions and philosophies. In another example, The Ritz-Carlton Hotel, known for superior customer service, launched a comprehensive program of quality management of the organization although with a clear statement that reads that the hotel is a place where the genuine care and comfort of their guests is their highest mission. Indeed, mission statements communicate a clear corporate culture, philosophy, and strategy (Baetz & Bart 1996).

Strategic Management

The design of a firm's mission statement includes many different viewpoints. An effective mission statement defines the fundamental, unique purpose that sets a business apart from other firms of its type, and identifies the scope of the business's operations in product and market terms (Pearce & David 1987). Setting goals and mission for a business is an integral part of the strategic management process and possibly the most visible public component (Pearce 1981). However, developing a mission statement is not the only component in the strategic management process of a firm to be successful. It needs to be aware of the environment in which it operates, the threats it can encounter, and the opportunities it can present (Wood 1983). Developing a strategy for a firm depends on the competitive environment and pressures. Pressures associated with international strategy formulation could be industry-specific such as the pressure to reduce costs; country-specific such as the cultural differences and trade barriers among countries; and company-specific pressures such as an organizational resistance to change (Beamish, Morrison, Inkpen, & Rosenzweig 2003). However, the best strategy is only as good as its implementation. One of the most significant challenges is to align a firm with a common direction (Slaaen 2012). Indeed, strategic thinking requires a manager to analyze the external environment from both a global and national perspective and develop goals based on an organization's mission and vision (Taneja, Pryor, Humphreys, & Singleton 2013).

Mission statements play an important role in business planning. Thus, mission statements historically also reflect the strategic planning process in firms such as nonprofits (Busch & Folaron 2005), professional practices (Kenyon & Brown 2007), secondary schools (Doolittle, Horner, Bradley,

Sugai, & Vincent 2007), for-profit corporations (Williams 2008), and university departments or schools (Stearns & Borna 1998), among others. Without the use of mission statements, consumers and stakeholders would not be supportive and loyal to companies, because of their lack of knowledge about organizational goals and values. Strategic planning begins with identification of the organization's mission so that stakeholders can be aligned with the organization's desired direction (Drucker 1973). Because mission statements define the nature, purpose, and role of organizations and focus resources and guide planning (Keeling 2013), contents of mission statements of luxury and ordinary brands may be expected to resemble each other, because both kinds of organizations must be competitive in the marketplace, and thus must have a strategy for the management of brands. A strong mission statement both inspires and challenges employees. It can make employees feel that they are part of something important, a vital operating principle for superior business performance. Mission statements and business performance are related (Baetz & Kenneth 1998).

Business Performance

Strategic planning leads to more rationality in the decision process, more involvement of team members in that process, and an increased possibility to share rich information, which enhances firm performance (Song, Im, Bij, & Song 2011). Corporate values such as innovation, fairness, and equity is related to organizational success (Ledford, Wendenhof, & Strahley 1995). This is why these values or philosophies are often stated publicly and included in mission statements that are used as a guide for gaining commitment to organizational goals and values (Gibson, Newton, & Cochran 1990). Firms that engage in strategic planning more easily could tackle and capitalize on the external environment than those firms that did not actively engage in strategic planning (Al-Shammari & Hussein 2007). In fact, it is found that if one of the purposes of strategic planning is to guide the organization in its relationships with the environment (Snow & Hambrick 1980), then organizations that accurately project and anticipate environmental changes should exhibit a far superior level of performance (Shrader, Taylor, & Dalton 1984). Theoretically, because the strategic planning aspect does not relate to status or emotions, etc., it can be argued that strategic management tactics and activities can be similar, if not the same, for both luxury and ordinary brands as both sets of brands operate and compete in the same competitive environment. However, in reality, these two sets of brands may not have similar strategic management tactics, as their marketing strategy and brand management need to be different to compete in the different target segments—demographics, psychographics, and international.

Further, the difference in marketing strategies of luxury and ordinary brands is the tactics they use to be different: traditional marketing frameworks view consumers as rational decision-makers focused on the functional features and benefits of products, whereas experiential marketing views consumers of luxury as emotional beings, focused on achieving pleasurable experiences (Atwal & Williams 2009). Therefore, if the marketing strategy is different for luxury and ordinary brands, it can be argued that strategic planning as a whole, including vision and mission, of luxury brands should be also different.

Conclusion

Mission statements are philosophical beliefs of a firm that it wishes to embody. It conveys a firm's winning idea or approach that sets them apart from competitors and also serves as an important tool for managers to assert their leadership within the organization. Business managers can use clearly developed mission and vision statements to communicate their intention and motivate their teams or organization to realize an inspiring common vision of the future. Although luxury brands are typically associated with money, status, and quality, consumers of luxury products usually purchase based on their perceptions of the brand image and the values and message it conveys to the stakeholders—internal or external—through the mission statements. As such, luxury brands need to establish trustful, mutually respectful, long-term relationships with the buyers to sustain and grow.

Experiential Learning

1. Visit the websites of at least 50 top luxury brands and 50 ordinary brands in terms of sales and compare contents of their mission statements using keywords (e.g. emotion, innovation, environment, etc.). After finding the keywords and collecting the data for both sets of brands, use at least a t-test to compare for statistical differences between the sets of mission statements across the keywords. Twenty sample luxury brand mission statements are presented in the appendix. The free content analysis tool can be used for the content analysis: www.catscanner.net
2. Split the data across luxury categories such as car, bags, jewelry, or whatever you like and run statistical tests to test differences in the mission statement contents.
3. Similarly, test if you find any difference in mission statements across countries or regions that have different cultures. Use the Hofstede score to determine cultural differences across the countries or regions.

References

Abelman, R. & Dalessandro, A. 2009. Institutional vision in Christian higher education: A Comparison of ACCU, ELCA, and CCCU Institutions. *Journal of Research on Christian Education*, 18(1), 84–119.

Al-Shammari, H.A. & Hussein, R.T. 2007. Strategic planning-firm performance linkage: Empirical investigation from an emergent market perspective. *Advances in Competitiveness Research*, 15–26.

Angriawan, A., Barczyk, C.C., Firlej, K., Rarick, C. & Nickerson, I. 2010. *A comparative study of U.S. and Chinese corporate mission statements*. Stockton, CA: International Academy of Business and Economic.

Atwal, G. & Williams, A. 2009. Luxury brand marketing: The experience is everything! *Journal of Brand Management, 16*(5/6), 338–346.

Baetz, B. & Kenneth, C. 1998. The relationship between mission statements and firm performance: An exploratory study. *Journal of Management Studies, 35*(6), 823–853.

Baetz, M.C. & Bart, C.K. 1996. Developing mission statements which work. *Long Range Planning, 29*(4), 526–533.

Bartkus, B.R., Glassman, M. & McAfee, R.B. 2004. A comparison of the quality of European, Japanese and US mission statements: A content analysis. *European Management Journal, 22*(4), 393–401.

Beamish, P.W., Morrison, A.J., Inkpen, A.C. & Rosenzweig, P.M. 2003. *International management: Text and cases*. International strategy implementation. Canada: McGrawHill.

Beverland, M. & Luxton, S. 2005. Managing Integrated Marketing Communication (IMC) through strategic decoupling: How luxury wine firms retain brand leadership while appearing to be wedded to the past. *Journal of Advertising, 34*(4), 103–116.

Bolon, D.S. 2005. Comparing mission statement content in for-profit and not-for-profit hospitals: Does mission really matter? *Hospital Topics, 83*(4), 2–9.

Busch, M. & Folaron, G. 2005. Accessibility and clarity of state child welfare agency mission statements. *Child Welfare, 84*(3), 415–430.

Cailleux, H.M., Mignot, C. & Kapferer, J.N. 2009. Is CRM for luxury brands? *Journal of Brand Management, 16*(5/6), 406–412.

Collins, J.C. & Porras, J.I. 1996. Building your company's vision. *Harvard Business Review, 74,* 65–77.

David, F. 1989. How companies define their mission. *Long Range Planning, 22*(1), 90–97.

Doolittle, J.H., Horner, R.H., Bradley, R., Sugai, G. & Vincent, C.G. 2007. Importance of student social behavior in the mission statements, personnel preparation standards, and innovation efforts of State departments of education. *Journal of Special Education, 40,* 239–245.

Drucker, P. 1973. *Management: Tasks, responsibilities, and practices*. New York: Harper & Row.

Dubois, B. & Paternault, C. 1995. Observations: Understanding the world of international luxury brands: The 'dream formula'. *Journal of Advertising Research, 35*(4), 69–76.

Farfan, B. 2018. The mission statements of luxury retail brands. www.thebalancesmb.com/retail-luxury-brands-mission-statement-2891761 [Accessed on July 2, 2020].

Firmin, M.W. & Gilson, K.M. 2009. Mission statement analysis of CCCU member institutions. *Journal of Christian Higher Education, 9*(1), 60–70.

Gibson, C.K., Newton, D.J. & Cochran, D.S. 1990. An empirical investigation of the nature of hospital mission statements. *Health Care Management Review, 15*(3), 35–45.

Ireland, D. & Hitt, M.A. 1992. Mission statements: Importance, challenge. *Business Horizons, 35*(3), 34.

Keeling, M. 2013. Mission statements: Rhetoric, reality, or road map to success? *Knowledge Quest, 42*(1), 30–36.

Kenyon, C.F. & Brown, J.B. 2007. Mission statement day: The impact on medical students of an early exercise in professionalism. *Medical Teacher*, 29(6), 606–610.

Kim, Y.K. & Sullivan, P. 2019. Emotional branding speaks to consumers' hearts: The case of fashion brands. *Fashion and Textiles*, 6(1).

Klemm, M., Sanderson, S. & Luffman, G. 1991. Mission statements: Selling corporate values to employees. *Long Range Planning*, 24(3), 73–78.

Ledford Jr., G.E., Wendenhof, J.R. & Strahley, J.T. 1995. Realizing a corporate philosophy. *Organizational Dynamics*, 23(3), 5–19.

Page, V. 2020. The psychology behind why people buy luxury goods. www.investo pedia.com/articles/personal-finance/091115/psychology-behind-why-people-buy-luxury-goods.asp [Accessed on July 2, 2020].

Patrick, P.G., Matthews, C.E., Ayers, D. & Tunnicliffe, S. 2007. Conservation and education: Prominent themes in zoo mission statements. *Journal of Environmental Education*, 38(3), 53–60.

Pearce II, J.A. 1981. An executive-level perspective on the strategic management process. *California Management Review*, 24(1), 39–48.

Pearce II, J.A. & David, F. 1987. Corporate mission statements: The bottom line. *Academy of Management Executive*, 1(2), 109–116.

Peyrefitte, J. & David, F.R. 2006. A content analysis of the mission statements of united states firms in four industries. *International Journal of Management*, 23(2), 296–301.

Schade, M., Hegner, S., Horstmann, F. & Brinkmann, N. 2016. The impact of attitude functions on luxury brand consumption: An age-based group comparison. *Journal of Business Research*, 69(1), 314–322.

Shrader, C.B., Taylor, L. & Dalton, D.R. 1984. Strategic planning and organizational performance: A critical appraisal. *Journal of Management*, 10(2), 149–171.

Slaaen, E. 2012. The best strategy is only as good as its implementation. *People & Strategy*, 35(4), 7–8.

Smith, M., Heady, R.B., Carson, P.P. & Carson, K.D. 2001. Do missions accomplish their missions? An exploratory analysis of mission statement content and organizational longevity. *Journal of Applied Management and Entrepreneurship*, 6, 75–96.

Snow, C.C., & Hambrick, D.C. 1980. Measuring organizational strategies: Some theoretical and methodological problems. *Academy of Management Review*, 5(4), 527–538.

Song, M., Im, S., Bij, H. & Song, L.Z. 2011. Does strategic planning enhance or impede innovation and firm performance? *Journal of Product Innovation Management*, 28, 503–520.

Stearns, J.M. & Borna, S. 1998. Mission statements in business higher education: Issues and evidence. *Higher Education Management*, 10(1), 89–104.

Straker, K. & Wrigley, C. 2018. From a mission statement to a sense of mission: Emotion coding to strengthen digital engagements. *Journal of Creating Value*, 4(1), 82–109.

Taneja, S., Pryor, M.G., Humphreys, J.H. & Singleton, L.P. 2013. Strategic management in an era of paradigmatic chaos: Lessons for managers. *International Journal of Management*, 30(1), 112–126.

Williams, L.S. 2008. The mission statement. *Journal of Business Communication*, 2, 94–119.

Wood, E.J. 1983. Strategic planning and the marketing process: Library applications. *Journal of Academic Librarianship*, 9(1), 15.

Woodside, A. & Fine, M. 2019. Sustainable fashion themes in luxury brand storytelling: The sustainability fashion research grid. *Journal of Global Fashion Marketing*, *10*(2), 111–128.

Wright, J.N. 2002. Mission and reality and why not? *Journal of Change Management*, *3*(1), 30–44.

Yeung, S.M.C. 2013. Application of six sigma and quality management ideas to the development of business school mission statements: A content analysis. *International Journal of Management*, *30*(2), 522–535.

Younghee, S., Won-Moo, H. & Minsung, K. 2012. Brand trust and affect in the luxury brand-customer relationship. *Social Behavior & Personality: An International Journal*, *40*(2), 331–338.

Zandstra, A.M. 2012. Mission statements of Christian elementary schools in the United States and the Netherlands. *Journal of Research on Christian Education*, *21*(2), 116–131.

Appendix

1. *Audi*: We delight customers worldwide. The Audi Group further defines what *customer delight* means with these four *actions*: We define innovation; We create experiences; We live responsibility; We shape Audi.
2. *Blancpain*: To provide our customers with the finest jewelry, timepieces, and accessories available with an emphasis on style and an incomparable eye for detail.
3. *BMW*: The BMW Group is the world's leading provider of premium products and premium services for individual mobility.
4. *Breitling*: We make watches for pilots who wear them as a badge of honor. And we make them for all the rugged individualists who dream of flying a fighter jet, but will settle for driving the fastest.
5. *Cadillac*: Cadillac will lead the luxury segment by offering must-have products that are professionally marketed, and delivered through a premium retail channel obsessed with customer satisfaction and sales/service.
6. *Chanel*: To be the Ultimate House of Luxury, defining style and creating desire, now and forever.
7. *Chopard*: As a family-owned luxury watch and jewelry manufacturer with a worldwide presence, we are honored to interact with our community and nurture the art of excellence and innovation with the highest respect for tradition.
8. *Christian Dior*: We strive to create an environment that is fun, welcoming and that encourages customers to tap into their creativity and explore their lifestyles. We strive to provide our clients with the highest quality promotional merchandise available worldwide.
9. *Christian Louboutin*: To make shoes that are like jewels.
10. *Clive Christian*: Create pure perfumes in complex formulas with the most precious natural ingredients from the corners of the British Empire.
11. *Hermès*: We believe by focusing on our performance and achieving excellence in customer service we will create a rewarding atmosphere for all of our stakeholders; creating a culture of repeat clientele, and leading us to be both an employer and partner of choice.
12. *Jimmy Choo*: Capture the hearts of women and inspire men around the world, to create exclusive shoes and accessories that are both luxurious

and practical for all occasions whilst creating a look instantaneously recognized as *Jimmy Choo*.

13. *Louis Vuitton*: Our savoir-faire, creativity and passion are revealed in all our activities: from the leather goods to jewelry, from ready-to-wear to shoes. The excellence offered to our customers every day is the result of a collective effort guided by values rooted in our history and transmitted for over 150 years.

14. *Mercedes-Benz*: Every call is a challenge. Every task is a chance to grow. Our vision is to become the world's most renowned center for customer service in the automotive sector. To meet our goal we are doing everything to create the best environment for skilled people from all over the world. Because only the best people can provide the best customer service. Ultimately it's that simple: we want to delight and satisfy our customers and partners.

15. *Moët & Chandon*: To share the magic of champagne with the world.

16. *Perrier Jouet*: Infusing poetry and beauty into daily life.

17. *Prada*: Prada's individuality made it one of the industry's most influential fashion houses and the brand continued to grow its premium status throughout the 1990s and beyond.

18. *Swatch*: The mission statement of Swatch Group is making the world's best watches and catering for the widest customer demands.

19. *Tiffany*: To be the world's most respected and successful designer, manufacturer and retailer of the finest jewelry.

20. *Yves Saint Laurent*: To provide future generations with a sustainable, beautiful Earth where opportunities are open in their futures that past generations could only imagine. It intends to inspire, teach, learn, and explore every day of life.

Note: These random representative mission/vision/strategy statements—collected from various sources—are intended to stimulate debate in the classroom through discussion of issues relating to marketing and management of luxury and fashion products and services in the global business environment. The samples are not intended to illustrate the mission statements' or management's effectiveness or ineffectiveness in tackling the issues.

3 Logos

Introduction

Logos or similar terms have existed in literature since the late 19th century (Cervellon 2013). *Logo* refers to a distinct symbol of a company, object, publication, person, service, idea, or identity (Adams, Morioka, & Stone 2006). Logos contribute to brand equity and develop brand identity (Cohen 1986). Logos are an integral part of advertising and seen as contributing to intangible visual assets through brand equity (Klein 1999). Logos can also act as a means to express brand identity through a combination of typeface and graphic elements (Henderson & Cote 1998). The importance of typeface, when articulating a message to customers, cannot be underestimated. It is an important attribute of a logo. The right logo font is crucial to understanding how customers respond emotionally to the logos (Henderson 2005). Consumers interpret messages based on logo designs. A good logo design should induce a decent level of recognition and familiarity with the company, convey the intended message to their target segment, and evoke positive emotions (Wang, Duff, & Clayton 2018). Logo design also affects whether consumers perceive the brand as being modern or not (Müller, Kocher, & Crettaz 2011). Certain logo characteristics can explain the attitude of customers towards logos, brand loyalty, and identity. Logos draw attention, communicate messages, and generate feelings and convince consumers to patronize the business. A well-designed and loved logo is particularly important for customers of luxury products and services, as some customers adore the brand identity and are willing to suffer in its name (Banks 2012). The key component of brand identity provides instant recognition for the brand and helps transcend international boundaries and language barriers because they communicate visually (Kohli, Suri, & Thakor 2002). Because brand identity is influenced by logos, so when done correctly, it can lead to superior business performance (Olins 1990). Logos contribute to brand equity and help consumers with brand recognition and differentiation. Often, logos are considered a part of a brand development exercise (Cohen 1986). A distinct logo design has distinguishing effects on brands that can stimulate emotional reactions and trigger brand recognition and memories (Chadwick & Walters 2009; Hollis 2005). Emotional attachment and perception of luxury logos are important factors for customers to expresses themselves socially (Zhang, Jin, Wang, Ma, & Yu 2019). Logos are company assets. In the next section, we explain a few logo design concepts.

Symbol

The symbolic role of luxury brands plays in consumers lives (Belk 1988). The brand symbolism—perceived or actual—relates to who the brand is and where it is from (Thurlow & Aiello 2007). A symbol is an arbitrary design with a meaning attached to it. For example, a red cross (arbitrary art or design) symbolizes hospital (meaning). Companies use the same concept when designing a logo and associating it with a message (e.g. beauty, simplicity, ethics, etc.). Symbolic interactionism explains how we give certain meaning to objects, and how our interactions with others determine the meaning of our reality. For example, for most of us, the well-known luxury brand Louis Vuitton (LV) logo signifies style, status, and sophistication. But how did we attach a meaning to it? In fact, we have our own thoughts on certain symbols within society, and we give meaning to these luxury logos by giving them status through our interactions with others (Shank & Lulham 2016). And because social status depends on others' willingness to grant it, social emulation is normally overt. Purchasing luxury products for status is public (Truong & Rod 2011). So meaning of the symbol as logo in this instance depends on society and its interactions with people. Indeed, the LV logo is simple, yet it symbolizes status. Most luxury brands have a symbolic meaning, mission, or philosophy to their logos.

Logos also symbolize the past, present, and future of a business. Managing corporate reputation and brand image is important. Logos can serve as a positive or negative reminder of the company's history. Customers should be able to identify companies' logos with their businesses instantly. A company's survival may depend on developing and maintaining a recognizable image and favorable reputation (Gray & Balmer 1998). If a luxury brand has been successful in delivering consistently excellent products and services, without falling into controversies such as use of animal cruelty, environment degradation, etc., their logos may symbolize positive aspects of the companies. Usually, luxury brands are positive reminders to their consumers.

Shape

One of the aesthetic features of logo design is its shape (Brading & Castellani 2003). A memorable and recognizable shape of a logo is essential for luxury brands. Shapes along with symmetry of a logo may render an understanding of the brand image. A diagonal or angular shape may be perceived as threat, whereas a round shape or curves may be perceived as pleasant (Wong 1993). Naturally, shapes trigger emotions and feelings towards logos. In the automobile category, luxury cars have different styles and shapes of logos that give consumers a distinct feeling of class and sophistication. The majority of luxury car logos seem to be circular (indicating friendliness, balance, harmony, etc.) or feature animals (suggesting power, speed, restlessness, etc.). Audi, BMW, Mercedes, Jaguar, etc., render a sense of connection, community, and friendliness. However, other luxury brands such as Bentley, Cadillac, Maserati, Rolls Royce, etc., have different shapes. Yet, the logo for another luxury brand, Lamborghini, is angular and has sharp edges and a bull at the center, signifying bullfighting—a threatening emotion. However, the bull in the logo also signifies the tremendous power of the engine and may symbolize success, wealth, and high class—all the positives that customers desire to display their accomplishments. Most logo designs appear to include multiple features—square, triangle, and animal—as in the case of Ferrari. Similarities of these features can also be found in ordinary brands. Regardless, shapes and symbols give meaning to consumers to determine how intense the need is to own the brand that will boost their economic status. A distinguishable logo within society enables the brand to be more sought after, as consumers want others to notice and recognize the higher status they have by owning the brand.

Size

Usually, luxury logos are relatively small. They are used to inform people who are less familiar with the brand. As such, rich customers do not need to display their wealth through logos, because they have status already; they buy luxury products for their quality and heritage. However, other customers may buy luxury brands for their symbolic and social value rather than inherent utility (Cavender 2018). By noticeably displaying luxury brands, these customers may need a sense of superiority to feel special, because they are one of the few who can afford to purchase the product (Garfein 1989; Hennigs, Wiedmann, & Klarmann 2012). Determining luxury logo size seems to be challenging, as luxury brands such as Chanel, Furla, and LV, among others, use smaller logos or even in some cases no logos at all. Yet, the brands can be identified by the unique design and pattern of their products only. Contrarily, inexpensive brands (e.g. H&M, Zara, Michael Kors, etc.) seem to have larger and more noticeable logos, appealing to customers who may have a pronounced need to signal their status, power, success, and wealth, among other qualities. A difference in logo size can also be observed in the Mercedes car, for example. It seems that the relatively "inexpensive" Mercedes C Series has a larger logo in the front compared with its expensive flagship model—S Series. In any case, logos should be clear, decent, and comprehensible in all sizes and in all formats—print and electronic.

Color

Logo color is a physical characteristic that sways consumers' perceptions and reactions to brands, products, or organizations. Colors' aesthetic appearance can affect the cognition, mood, and behavior of people (Elliot & Maier 2014;

Singh 2006). Color serves as the *silent salesperson* that exerts persuasive power at a subliminal level (Hynes 2009). Therefore, logo color can shape consumer perceptions, as it carries intrinsic meaning that becomes central to the brand identity and image and its recognition. The extrinsic feature of logos such as colors embodies the intrinsic meaning of what the business would like to portray. Thus, luxury brands with sensory-social images are better received in red and black or a subdued color such as dark blue, black, red, gray, or purple (Bottomley & Doyle 2006). A positive relationship exists between competence and the color blue, and a positive relationship between sophistication and black and purple colors (Labrecque & Milne 2012). Air France, Chanel, and the University of Oxford, among other entities, use dark colors. The Four Seasons' primarily black logo denotes luxury. However, blue is also found to be associated with wealth, trust, and security, and gray with strength and exclusivity, whereas orange with cheapness (Madden, Hewett, & Roth 2000). Contrarily, ordinary brands tend to use lighter and brighter colors such as yellow, orange, light blue, pink, and green (Hynes 2009). Ordinary brands (e.g. IKEA, McDonald's, WestJet, and Super 8 Motels, among others) use bright colors. Inexpensive fast food restaurants (e.g. A&W) also generally use a bright color (e.g. A&W orange) logos. Indeed, communication, marketing, and retail sectors acknowledge the role of color in getting attention, inducing mood, or conveying complex information to achieve specific goals (Seraphin, Ambaye, Gowreesunkar, & Bonnardel 2016). Color can also be used in a tactical way to alter brand personality and persuade consumers to buy or switch (Labrecque & Milne 2012).

Simplicity and Complexity

Simplicity refers to the minimal use of elements in design. The minimalistic nature of logos aids cleanness, easy recall, and clarity in message, leading to brand recognition. Simple logos are easily memorizable, as they require less information-processing capacity. These logos are suitable for all platforms—print and electronic. Most luxury logos are simple and memorable so much so that brand names are just written in a font as text. However, there is also evidence that complex logos are effective in garnering brand recognition (Foo 2003). Logo *complexity* refers to elaborateness, arising from design features such as number of elements used, irregularity in arrangement of elements, and ornamental nature of the design (Henderson & Cote 1998). Complex logos can also be effective, because they may have more potential for arousal, which increases cognitive processing time. The increased exposure to complex logos increases likeability, which in turn leads to brand recognition (Van Grinsven & Das 2015). The complex nature of such logos gives rise to creativity, expressiveness, and attractiveness, which can render a professional image of the company, thus making it unlikely to be forgotten. Versace is an excellent example of a company that has complex patterns in its logo that suggest creativity, colorfulness, and modernity. Complex logos may evoke confusion as well. The intended message of the logo may not be understood in a complex one. On the other hand, the Franck Muller logo is at least simple, yet it makes the most complicated watches in the world. Its tagline is "master of complications"!

Message

Luxury brands bring joy and prestige to consumers even though the same utility can be performed by inexpensive brands (Husic & Cicic 2009). Luxury brands have a well-known identity and enjoy high brand awareness and perceived quality through which they convey a clear, concerted, and consistent message to customers and the public. Consumer preferences, technology, and management change over time. These changes need to be communicated to customers. Companies do so usually by modifying elements of logos to reposition and convey a new message to consumers (Keller 2003). Consumer sensitivities to logos are positively related to brand performance (Stafford, Tripp, & Bienstock 2004). Logos can be detrimental to brand image if the modified logos do not represent accurately the message of the company or brand. GAP tried to modify and refresh its logo in 2010 but faced criticism from the public for its lack of details. Similalry, BP tried to reposition itself as a green company by modifying its logo as green but faced similar backlash. In another instance, when Tropicana juice changed its logo from an orange with an inserted straw to a glass of juice with a straw, consumers did not seem to like the change in the logo emotionally, forcing the brand to revert to the original logo. This explains why the Mercedes logo conveys a different message from the BMW logo even though both brands have similar features. Indeed, logos should reflect the brand message and spirit and differentiate themselves (Levin 1993). In some cases, customers are so connected with some logos that the logos have turned into icons (e.g. Coca-Cola, Xerox, LV, among others).

During the 2020 COVID-19 pandemic, it is interesting that brands such as Audi and Volkswagen communicated a *social distancing* message with their redesigned temporary logos. The term *social distancing* refers to a policy of being 6 feet apart from others to lower the risk of contracting the novel coronavirus. However, not everybody appreciated the social distancing logo. Brands that design social distancing logos may not have the potential to diminish the severity of the virus, but the creativity and passion, and the wish to help, educate, and be part of the physical distancing movement, is a noteworthy endeavor (Sellers 2020). Other brands also communicated to society without modifying their logos; for example, GAP and Ralph Lauren made masks for healthcare workers, whereas Christian Dior and Givenchy manufactured hand sanitizers (Valinsky 2020).

Implied Attributes

Implied logo attributes relate to what comes to our mind when we see a logo. If we look at the Alexander Keith brand's logo, which features a deer at the center, it conjures the images of wilderness and ruggedness—Canadian outdoorsy charm—in our mind. Consumers are more likely to buy brands from a country they like (Wang 2018). Indeed, it is Canadian brand. The more closely a brand and its image relate to how the consumer sees him or herself (or their ideal selves), the more likely the consumer is to favor or become loyal to that brand (Han 2005; Han & Back 2008). It is important to note that brand design and image are not limited to the logo itself but can *bleed* (e.g. extend the color schemes and motifs of their logo) into other product lines. Therefore, the product itself should exude some quality or attribute that can be linked to the brand and its logo (Rondeau 2005). This can also refer to the concept of branded house (e.g. Apple, FedEx, Google, Marriott, etc.). Buying a brand for its image, personality, or attributes is the main reason for choosing or switching (Melewar & Saunders 1998).

Culture

Different cultures respond to different colors as they carry different meanings. Green and white are universally liked and have similar meanings. Black and red are also universally liked, but the meaning varies across cultures (Madden, Hewett, & Roth 2000). Blue is the most preferred color in general across cultures (Wiegersma & Loon 1989). Orange is the most sacred color for Hindus in India, but the Ndembo in Zambia do not even acknowledge orange as a color. Muslims view green as a sacred color. For the Celts, green is a sacred color too, so they use it in marriages, whereas Christians use the color white in weddings as a symbol of purity and virginity. Although the color black is associated with negative connotations such as evil, death, and aggression, most luxury brands tend to use dark colors (Caldwell & Burger 2011; Frank & Gilovich 1988; Lakens, Semin, & Foroni 2012). Consumers of luxury brands infer that prestigious products should have dark colors (Rook & Levy 1983). It can be challenging to align a logo's color with the company's image given cultural differences. In an attempt to reposition as a global company, British Airways attempted to use traditional *British* colors and symbolism for various ethnic influences from around the world. But the attack by people and media on *Britishness* and its tradition left the company with financial losses (Thurlow & Aiello 2007). Because different cultures attach different meanings to colors, the right choice of colors in logos is important to achieve a sustained image of a brand in a customer's mind.

Culture informs logo design. Cultural beliefs such as the preference for rhythm, symmetry, unity, and harmony, among other elements, determine an effective logo design (Koffka 1962). Collectivistic cultures may like proportional and symmetrical logos, whereas individualistic cultures prefer iconic logos (Henderson, Cote, Leong, & Schmitt 2003). The degree of individualism in a society is a key factor to consider when designing an aesthetic strategy (Hofstede 1994). Individualistic societies such as Australia or America stress the creativity of its individuals, whereas collectivistic societies such as China or Japan stress social harmony (Schmitt & Simonson

1997). Therefore, we can expect iconoclastic design to be of greater value in an individualistic society than in a collectivistic one. Similarly, harmony and peace are preferred aesthetic expressions in a collectivistic society, where symbolism relating to discord is avoided (de Mooij 2005). Squares and triangles show stability and balance; triangles tend to be viewed as masculine and powerful; and circles suggest love and femininity (MDG 2015). Historically, logos were developed according to European tradition, culture, and styles (Carls 1989; Nelissen & Meijers 2011). However, preferences for design are far more universal than previously thought (Pittard 2007).

Sound

A *sound logo* refers to an identifying acoustic element of a brand with a 1- to 3-second running time. Sound logos may be combined with a visual logo using melody or a rhythm (Bronner 2008). When acoustic stimuli are used in advertising, they are experienced holistically, so the sound is interpreted along with the entire advertisement (Kellaris, Cox, & Cox 1993; Macinnis & Park 1991). Sound logos may positively affect consumers, if the music is commensurate with the nature of the luxury products. Because a logo is a visual representation of a company's identity or message, visually impaired people may not see it, in which case, the physical attribute of the logo loses its value, but the sound attribute of the logo may offset more than the loss. So, a sound logo without visuals can still be equally effective. In the US alone, the number of people with visual impairment or blindness is expected to be eight million by 2050. More than 16 million Americans are expected to have myopia (nearsightedness) or hyperopia (farsightedness), though this is correctable by eyeglasses, contacts, or surgery (NIH 2020). Although the use of sound symbols is relatively low in advertising, the need for sound logos in the future appears to be high.

Effectiveness

An effective logo has a high degree of naturalness, media exposure, and subdued images to increase brand recognition (Landry 1998). Logos can benefit a company, as they are easily and quickly received and perceived compared with words. Even the shortest exposure results in a message being received and understood, increasing brand recognition (Henderson, Cote, Leong, & Schmitt 2003). On the contrary, it has also been found that the use of logos may be temporary and unnecessary. For example, an advertisement's attraction value does not increase when a logo is present compared with when it is absent, and the intended effect of the advertisement does not increase when a logo is present compared with when it is absent (Decrop 2007). That is, the presence of logos may not influence consumers as much as marketers believe. Some high-end brands have reached a point where they can be recognized without logos. The status needs of different segments are different.

High-status, affluent people may not feel the need to show their wealth or prove themselves to the rest of the population (Kapferer 2010). As such, luxury brands resist popularizing their logos as the logos lose their luxury value (Han, Nunes, & Dreze 2010). Different social goals that consumers want to achieve through luxury consumption allow consumers to express themselves (a value-expressive function) or present themselves (a social-adjusted function) in front of others (Zhang, Jin, Wang, Ma, & Yu 2019). Having logos and not having logos fulfill both functions and can be effective in delivering their respective messages.

No Logos

No-logo products refer to those that do not have a brand name or logo on them, or at least not in an obvious spot, or hidden. The brand instead sells itself based on its features. Consumers can identify luxury brands by their pattern of design rather than their logo display. The unique checks of Burberry, colors of brands such as LV or Ferrari, or even the distinct sound of Harley Davidson are sufficient for customers of intended segments to associate these characteristics with brands without the presence of logos on the products. The look, feel, and design of such products should be an indication of their high-quality, luxury nature. Because no-logo brands need to be recognized instantly, unique designs and their virtual association with logos are paramount. Customers of no-logo brands are more concerned with quality and design than with the need for logo display. What follows are a few arguments for no logos.

Why No Logos

Exclusivity

The no-logo strategy is intended to create a sense of exclusivity by offering high-quality products to customers. This strategy appears to reduce general brand visibility particularly in emerging markets of Asia and, to some extent, Africa, where luxury products are becoming more accessible. High-status consumers purchase significantly expensive and subtle luxury items that do not tend to display prominent logos. In these cases, anonymity can create even more prestige (Avins 1996). Such consumers place more emphasis on quality, craftsmanship, and timelessness associated with luxury products. Because they already have status, power, and wealth, there is seldom a need to exhibit superiority through loud logos. These consumers seem to be moving towards purchasing luxury products with no, minimal, or hidden logos. This behavior allows them to distance themselves from those, for example, who cannot afford original products and who thus resort to counterfeit products, which usually do feature prominent logos.

Counterfeit

Consumers may purchase counterfeit luxury products to create an identity for themselves as being among the few who can afford to live the luxurious life. Therefore, the circulation of counterfeit luxury products is detrimental to luxury brand image and exclusive value. With the rise in counterfeit products, luxury brands risk losing profit and prestige when consumers outside of their target market display cheap, low-quality items with their logo on it, which dilutes the brand image. High-status consumers may not want to debate what are real versus counterfeit products and thus may just opt out of buying products with logos (Hennigs, Wiedmann, & Klarmann 2012). In this situation, no-logo products may serve this niche segment better. Indeed, luxury brands need a high-value niche segment.

Hierarchy

Society is hierarchical. People buy luxury products to fulfill psychological needs to fit into a certain stratum of society. If luxury brands collectively are able to attach a symbolic meaning to no-logo brands that they are for elite society, then there may be peer pressure among the wealthy to buy no-logo products, because they may not like to be included with other society members, who show off luxury items, thereby making them look less luxurious and diminishing the items' prestige and values. Joining upper society by buying no-logo products may suggest a certain level of emotional maturity, socially upward mobility, and conformity to new society-based standards. That is, only people in higher social classes will recognize features (e.g. fine stitches, pattern, texture, etc.) of the no-logo products, and people in lower social classes will not notice them because of their lack of knowledge about the product, quality, and heritage. Elite consumers are also more likely to have a personal relationship with the brand, because the brand is an extension of who they are, versus other consumers, who are only using the brand to portray a sense of high social status (Han, Nunes, & Dreze 2010).

Animals

Some of the most expensive and well-known luxury fashion brands (e.g. Burberry, Hermès, Prada, etc.) are known for using rare animals to make luxury products. It is possible that some consumers may adore the brands and yet do not want to be seen as supporting them (by having their logos on the products) because of the companies' controversial business practices. Certain associations that advocate for cruelty-free production, such as People for the Ethical Treatment of Animals (PETA), may not support the idea of animal cruelty for commercial gain. A no-logo brand could serve this luxury segment well. But the segment may be accused of hypocrisy.

Religion

Religious consumers appear to be more conservative and exhibit more conscious reactions to marketing than non-religious consumers (Leary, Minton, & Mittelstaesdt 2016). In this regard, equality and prejudices is a topic of discussion worldwide. The Coke brand wished to play a role in promoting harmony by removing the label from its cans during the month of Ramadan to promote a world without labels and prejudices. Coke removed its logos from its packaging in the Middle East to encourage people not to judge one another (O'Reilly 2015). The no-logo strategy can also serve as an effective communications tool.

Modesty

Last but not least, some consumers are just too humble, polite, and modest to use luxury products displaying logos. For them, it may mean a lack of empathy and humility. No-logo products may mitigate the feeling.

Marketing of No-Logo Products

No-logo products may require a word-of-mouth (WOM) marketing strategy. WOM strategy is based on a social network. Its structure is composed of actors (such as individuals or luxury brands who are represented by nods), and the relationship between them is the tie. WOM is expressed as passing information along the tie between two nods. The information eventually spreads from the nod that received the information to another new nod, and thus an information network is formed (Wasserman & Faust 2009). Social media facilitates WOM communications. No-logo products may also take advantage of celebrity endorsement.

Conclusion

The notion behind an effective logo is to develop consumers' recognition and recall of the company's brand. By creating a memorable image in consumers' minds, a company is able to establish a lasting impression on its current and potential customers. Companies do this by creating innovative logos and by attaching a message about what the company's brand stands for. The influence of innovation and creativity in logo design stimulates the consumer to recognize and identify a certain brand and its message. The more opportunities consumers have to recognize a brand, the more they will depend on that brand to satisfy their needs. However, the needs can also be satisfied without putting logos on products, in which case, the uniqueness and design of the product itself should be powerful enough for brand recognition and its subsequent performance.

Experiential Learning

1. Locate the journal article provided here. Using the logo guidelines, compare 50 luxury logos with ordinary logos using the features indicated in the chapter such as shape, size, symmetry, etc.
   Henderson, P.W. & Cote, J.A. 1998. Guidelines for selecting or modifying logos. *Journal of Marketing*, 62, 14–30.
   For the logo database, visit: www.1000logos.net
2. Visit the following site and discover hidden design and messages in the famous logos. Then design a fictitious logo with your message for a brand in a particular luxury category (e.g. fashion, car, jewelry, etc.).
   www.cnn.com/style/article/hidden-designs-famous-logos/index.html
3. Visit the following website and get some ideas how to optimize logos to use less ink to make them more eco-friendly (i.e. eco logos). The eco logos themselves convey the message that the company is environmentally friendly. Optimize any three logos of your choice in the luxury category. Explain how the newly designed logo is eco-friendly.
   www.boredpanda.com/less-ink-ecobranding-logo-design

References

Adams, S., Morioka, N. & Stone, T.L. 2006. *Logo design workbook: A hands-on guide to creating logos*. Rockport, MA: Rockport Publishers.

Avins, M. 1996. Labels make comeback as symbols sans status. *Orange County Edition: Los Angeles Times*.

Banks, T. 2012. Should brands have a single logo or an adaptable identity? *Design Week* (Online Edition), 3. https://www.designweek.co.uk/issues/may-2012/should-brands-have-a-single-logo-or-an-adaptable-identity [Accessed on September 17, 2020].

Belk, R. 1988. Possessions and the extended self. *Journal of Consumer Research*, 15(2), 139–168.

Bottomley, P.A. & Doyle, J.R. 2006. The interactive effects of colors and products on perceptions of brand logo appropriateness. *Marketing Theory*, 6(1), 63–83.

Brading, K. & Castellani, E. 2003. *Symmetries in physics: Philosophical reflections*. Cambridge, UK: Cambridge University Press.

Bronner, K. 2008. Jingle all the way? Basics of audio branding. In K. Bronner & R. Hirt (Eds.), *Audio branding: Brands, sound and communication* (pp. 77–87). Baden-Baden: Nomos Publisher.

Caldwell, D.F. & Burger, J.M. 2011. On thin ice: Does uniform color really affect aggression in professional hockey? *Social Psychological Personal Science*, 2(3), 306–310.

Carls, K 1989. Corporate coats of arms. *Harvard Business Review*, May/June, 135–139.

Cavender, R. 2018. The marketing of sustainability and CSR initiatives by luxury brands: Cultural indicators, call to action, and framework. In C. Lo & J. Ha Brookshire (Eds.), *Sustainability in luxury fashion business* (pp. 29–47). Singapore: Springer.

Cervellon, M.C. 2013. Conspicuous conservation: Using semiotics to understand sustainable luxury. *International Journal of Market Research*, 55(5), 695–717.

Chadwick, S. & Walters, G. 2009. Sportswear identification, distinctive design and manufacturer logos: Issues from the front line. *Marketing Review*, 9(1), 63–78.

Cohen, D. 1986. Trademark strategy. *Journal of Marketing*, 50, 61–74.

Decrop, A. 2007. The influence of message format on the effectiveness of print advertisements for tourism destinations. *International Journal of Advertising*, 26(4), 505–525.

de Mooij, M. 2005. *Global marketing and advertising: Understanding cultural paradoxes*. London: Sage.

Elliot, J. & Maier, M.A. 2014. Color psychology: Effects of perceiving color on psychological functioning in humans. *Annual Review of Psychology*, 65(1), 95–120.

Foo, C.T. 2003. Visualizing complexity in corporate identity on the internet: An empirical investigation. *Corporate Communications: An International Journal*, 8(1), 11–17.

Frank, M.G. & Gilovich, T. 1988. The dark side of self- and social-perception: Black uniforms and aggression in professional sports. *Journal of Personal Social Psychology*, 54(1), 74–85.

Garfein, R.T. 1989. Cross-cultural perspectives on the dynamics of prestige. *Journal of Marketing*, 3(3), 17–24.

Gray, E.R. & Balmer, J.M.T. 1998. Managing corporate image and corporate reputation. *Long Range Planning*, 33(5), 695–702.

Han, H. & Back, K.J. 2008. Relationships among image congruence, consumption emotions, and customer loyalty in the lodging industry. *Journal of Hospitality & Tourism Research*, 32(4), 467–490.

Han, H. 2005. Hotel restaurant co-branding: The relationship of perceived brand fit with intention to purchase. *Journal of Hospitality & Tourism Research*, 29(4), 48–467.

Han, Y.J., Nunes, J.C. & Dreze, X. 2010. Signalling status with luxury goods: The role of brand prominence. *Journal of Marketing*, 74, 15–30.

Henderson, P.W. 2005. Just my type. *Harvard Business Review*, 83(4), 22–23.

Henderson, P.W. & Cote, J.A. 1998. Guidelines for selecting or modifying logos. *Journal of Marketing*, 62, 14–30.

Henderson, P.W., Cote, J.A., Leong, S.M. & Schmitt, B. 2003. Building strong brands in Asia: Selecting the visual components of image to maximize brand strength. *International Journal of Research in Marketing*, 20, 297–313.

Hennigs, N., Wiedmann, K.P. & Klarmann, C. 2012. Consumer value perception of luxury goods: A cross-cultural and cross-industry comparison. *Luxury Marketing*, 77–99.

Hofstede, G. 1994. Management scientists are human. *Management Science*, 40, 4–13.

Hollis, N. 2005. Finding more like this: Branding unmasked. *Marketing Research*, 17(3), 24–29.

Husic, M. & Cicic, M. 2009. Luxury consumption factors. *Journal of Fashion Marketing and Management*, 13(2), 231–245.

Hynes, N. 2009. Colour and meaning in corporate logos: An empirical study. *Journal of Brand Management*, 16(8), 545–555.

Kapferer, N. 2010. Luxury after the crisis: Pro logo or no logo? *The European Business Review*, 43–44.

Kellaris, J.J., Cox, A.D. & Cox, D. 1993. The effect of background music on ad processing: A contingency explanation. *Journal of Marketing*, 57(Oct), 114–125.

Keller, K.L. 2003. Brand synthesis: The multidimensionality of brand knowledge. *Journal of Consumer Research*, 29(Mar), 595–600.

Klein, N. 1999. *No logo: No space, no choice, no job*. New York: Picador.

Koffka, K. 1962. *Principles of gestalt psychology*. London: Routledge.

Kohli, C., Suri, R. & Thakor, M. 2002. Creating effective logos: Insights from theory and practice. *Business Horizons*, May–June, 58–64.

Labrecque, L.I. & Milne, G.R. 2012. Exciting red and competent blue: The importance of color in marketing. *Academy of Marketing Science*, 40(5), 711–727.

Lakens, D., Semin, G.R. & Foroni, F. 2012. But for the bad, there would be no good: Grounding valence in brightness through shared relational structures. *Journal of Experimental Psychology*, 141, 584–594.

Landry, J.T. 1998. Making logos matter. *Harvard Business Review*, 76(2), 16–17.

Leary, R.B., Minton, E.A. & Mittelstaesdt, J.D. 2016. Thou shall not? The influence of religion on beliefs of stewardship and dominion, sustainable behaviors, and marketing systems. *Journal of Macromarketing*, 36(4), 1–14.

Levin, G. 1993. Some logos hurt brand image. *Advertising Age*, 64(38), 40.

Macinnis, D.J. & Park, C.W. 1991. The differential role of characteristics of music on high- and low-involvement consumers' processing of ads. *Journal of Consumer Research*, 18(2), 161–173.

Madden, T.J., Hewett, K. & Roth, M.S. 2000. Managing images in different cultures: A cross-national study of color meanings and preferences. *Journal of International Marketing*, 8(4), 90–107.

MDG Advertising. 2015. Discover how the look of your logo both colors and shapes perceptions. *Advertising and Marketing Blog*. www.mdgadvertising.com/blog/discover-how-the-look-of-your-logo-both-colors-and-shapes-perception-infographic [Accessed on July 2, 2020].

Melewar, T.C. & Saunders, J. 1998. Global corporate visual identity systems: Standardization, control and benefits. *International Marketing Review*, 15(4), 291–308.

Müller, B., Kocher, B. & Crettaz, A. 2011. The effects of visual rejuvenation trough brand logos. *Journal of Business Research*, 1–7.

Nelissen, R. & Meijers, M. 2011. Social benefits of luxury brands as costly signals of wealth and status. *Evolution and Human Behavior*, 32(5), 343–355.

NIH 2020. National Institutes of Health. www.nih.gov/news-events/news-releases/visual-impairment-blindness-cases-us-expected-double-2050 [Accessed on July 2, 2020].

Olins, W. 1990. In corporate identity: Making business strategy visible through design. *Harvard Business Review*, 68(5), 153–157.

O'Reilly, L. 2015. Business insider. www.businessinsider.com/coca-cola-removes-labels-from-cans-for-ramadan-campaign-2015-7 [Accessed on July 2, 2020].

Pittard, N., Ewing, M. & Jevons, C. 2007. Aesthetic theory and logo design: Examining consumer response to proportion across cultures. *International Marketing Review*, 24(4), 457–473.

Rondeau, D.B. 2005. For mobile applications, branding is experience. *Communications of the ACM*, 48(7), 61–66.

Rook, D.W. & Levy, S.J. 1983. Psychosocial themes in consumer grooming rituals. In R.P. Bagozzi & A.M. Tybout (Eds.), *Advances in consumer research volume 10* (pp. 329–333). Ann Abor, MI: Association for Consumer Research.

Schmitt, B.H. & Simonson, A. 1997. *Marketing aesthetics*. New York: The Free Press.

Sellers, D. 2020. Executive creative director, Siegel+Gale, CNN Business. https://www.news24.com/you/news/big-brands-revamp-their-logos-to-encourage-social-distancing-amid-coronavirus-20200401 [Accessed on September 17, 2020].

Seraphin, H., Ambaye, M., Gowreesunkar, V. & Bonnardel, V. 2016. A marketing research tool for destination marketing organizations' logo design. *Journal of Business Research*, 69(11), 5022–5027.

Shank, D.B. & Lulham, R. 2016. Symbolic interaction with consumer products: An affect control theory approach. *Sociology Compass, 10*(7), 613–622.

Singh, S. 2006. Impact of color on marketing. *Management Decision, 44*(6), 783–789.

Stafford, M.R., Tripp, C. & Bienstock, C.C. 2004. The influence of advertising logo characteristics on audience perceptions of nonprofit theatrical organizations. *Journal of Current Issues and Research in Advertising, 26*(1), 37–45.

Thurlow, C. & Aiello, G. 2007. National pride, global capital: A social semiotic analysis of transnational visual branding in the airline industry. *Visual Communication, 6*(3), 305–344.

Truong, Y. & Rod, M. 2011. Intrinsic motivations, self-esteem, and luxury goods consumption. *Journal of Retailing and Consumer Services, 18*(6), 555–561.

Valinsky, J. 2020. McDonald's and other brands are making social distancing logos. www.cnn.com/2020/03/26/business/social-distancing-brand-logos-coronavirus/index.html [Accessed on July 2, 2020].

Van Grinsven, B. & Das, E. 2015. Logo design in marketing communications: Brand logo complexity moderates exposure effects on brand recognition and brand attitude. *Journal of Marketing Communications, 22*(3), 256–270.

Wang, B., Duff, R.L. & Clayton, R.B. 2018. Establishing a factor model for aesthetic preference for visual complexity of brand logo. *Journal of Current Issues & Research in Advertising, 39*(1), 83–100.

Wang, J. 2018. Influence of brand logo on the neuropsychological mechanism of luxury goods price acceptance. *NeuroQuantology*, 478–482.

Wasserman, S. & Faust, K. 2009. *Social network analysis: Methods and applications.* Cambridge: Cambridge University Press.

Wiegersma, S. & Loon, A.V. 1989. Some variables in the blue (red) phenomenon. *Journal of General Psychology, 116*(3), 256–269.

Wong, W. 1993. *Principles of form and design.* New York: Van Nostrand Reinhold.

Zhang, W., Jin, J., Wang, A., Ma, Q. & Yu, H. 2019. Consumers' implicit motivation of purchasing luxury brands: An EEG study. *Psychology Research and Behavior Management, 12*, 913–929.

4   Airport Retailing and Franchising

Introduction

Airports are increasingly becoming more attractive to retailers. Airport retailing accounts for significant airport revenue. Nearly half of airports' income is generated by non-aeronautical activities. Retailing is responsible for 20 percent of the revenues at some of the busiest airports in the US (Appold & Kasarda 2006). Luxury products are in great demand at airport retail shops (Berry 1994). Stores at airports can generate annual sales of $800-$1,200 per square foot compared with $300 per square foot in an average regional mall in the US (ACINA 2005). As airports expand commercial activities, they are forced to adopt a marketing-oriented approach. Airports need to capitalize on the opportunities afforded to them and develop a range of segments and categories specific to the airport environment (Freathy & O'Connell 1999). The marketing-oriented approach has caused airports to be more concerned with their retail tenant mix (Bingman 1996). As a result, airports are becoming larger to facilitate more retail outlets. In fact, some of the international airport departure lounges resemble shopping malls in many countries (e.g. Panama, Hong Kong, etc.). The increase in commercial space positively affects revenue generation from the traveler. But having too much space devoted to retail stores can result in overcrowding of shoppers and consequently may decrease customer satisfaction. As such, airport retailing has become a much more sophisticated business in attracting luxury brands. Franchising at airports is one of the options for luxury brands to enter a new market with minimal risks and investments. In the next section, we cover airport environment, airport marketing, airport advertising, luxury retailing, impulse shoppers, and apathetic shoppers. The franchising section includes discussion of franchising strategy, franchising at airports, flagship luxury stores, corporate-owned luxury stores, pop-up stores, and luxury services.

Airport Environment

Traveling puts travelers in a unique environment at airports. It is much different from the normal retail environment. The environment can influence their purchasing behavior in a way the customers may not act as they usually do in their normal shopping environment (Crawford & Melewar 2003). Periods of anxiety, stress, and relaxation make up an unusual airport environment that creates a state of isolation from the references of their cultures, countries of origin, and any other preferences and specifications that they usually have in other retail environments. So, travelers experience feelings that lead to them reacting in unusual ways that differentiate them from a regular buyer in a normal situation (Lin & Chen 2013). Further, shopping is not the main reason for consumers to be at the airport. The airport environment contributes to two emotional factors—an increase in stress levels and an increase in levels of excitement and anticipation—that affect the buying habits of consumers in airport settings (Thomas 1997). However, after receiving their boarding passes, passengers experience a lower level of stress and a higher period of excitement. Customers now also realize that they have additional time before boarding their planes, so they are more likely to engage in browsing and impulse-buying behavior (Kennedy, Ferrell, & LeClaire 2001).

Airport terminals play an important role in segmenting customers based on their purchasing behaviors and patterns. When consumers travel through international airports, they are in a state of timelessness and spacelessness. They are almost captive, with nowhere to go until they board their next flight (Rowley & Slack 1999). This situation encourages browsing behavior that may result in impulse purchases (Slater & Olson 2001). However, travelers also experience psychological tension while at the airport, which can negatively affect their impulse purchasing. Further, airports are becoming larger, and therefore, the distance between passengers' check-in desk and boarding gate has increased, making travelers even more anxious and stressed. So, locating retail stores near the boarding gates, segmented by customers' needs and wants, can be an efficient way of encouraging unplanned purchases resulting from the more relaxed and less anxious atmosphere. Selling luxury products, using the advantage of a non-home atmosphere, and placing large, visual close-up advertisements to create an effective marketing environment at the airport is an opportunity for airport retailers.

Airport Marketing

Pre-boarding areas are most suitable for targeting travelers as they are more relaxed and prone to visiting shops. These areas are designed in such a way that consumers are able to shop in a store easily without having to go too far from their departure gates (Van Oel & Van den Berkhof 2013). Some airports segment stores by gates, where passengers from a specific country or income group are concentrated (Freathy & O'Connell 1999). This airport layout segmentation technique influences travelers' behavior while waiting to board their aircrafts. Layout segmentation has been proven to increase sales in the airport setting by alleviating stress and making shopping more convenient for consumers (Crawford & Melewar 2003). Terminals ensure optimal retail space utilization according to the needs of the travelers. Because different terminals have different traffic flows, international terminals usually have relatively large passenger traffic and thus use large-screen displays for advertising (Lloyd 2003). The importance of paying equal attention to the store design, lighting, color combination, and design of passenger pre-boarding areas according to cultural preferences and specifications cannot be underestimated. Shape of the roof and hallways and warmness and coolness of the lighting and colors contribute to comfort. Indeed, an optimal area balance is needed between commercial activities (revenue generation) and public facilities (service level) available at airports (Hsu & Chao 2005). The optimized pre-boarding area may make travelers feel comfortable and relaxed and thus increase their spending behavior. Brands can meet customers' preferences by determining their income, country of origin, and culture, for example. An airport is a niche area.

Airports collect travel-related data such as flight schedules, age, nationality, and consumer preferences (Newman & Lloyd-Jones 1999). Information gathered from flight schedules helps retailers target specific departure gates and merchandise their stores accordingly (e.g. Latin Americans like reading novels or Asians like to give gifts, etc.). Because of high anxiety levels, travelers like being close to their departure gates, so they could shop (Doganis 1992). The effective use of customer information can lead to customizing marketing activities and increasing business performance. If the airport environment is carefully marketed, airport retailers can change customers' idle time into shopping time (Omar & Kent 2001).

Airport Advertising

Advertising in the airport retail environment benefits from substantial levels of traffic and reach (Morgan & Pritchard 2004). Mass advertising can increase the incidence of impulse buying behavior (Stern 1962). Indoor advertising has become an important tool for airport retailers to increase their commercial revenues and create an effective marketing environment by incorporating digital advertising technologies. Luxury brands and stores use this tool to generate impulses in consumers by providing visual and promotional stimuli (Piron 1991). Consumers may experience an urge to buy impulsively when visually encountering cues such as promotional incentives (Dholakia 2000). Point-of-purchase techniques such as in-store settings, on-shelf positioning, samplings, point-of-purchase displays, and in-store demonstrations can significantly influence impulse buying (Yu & Bastin 2010). Another retail advertising technique that encourages impulse buying among travelers at airport retail shops is the innovative display of products, which emphasizes exclusive availability in the clean and spacious format of the store (Omar & Kent 2001). Therefore, different advertising techniques combined with emotions may excite customers to impulsively buy something even if it is not needed. However, caution needs to be exercised. Indoor airport advertisements may not influence consumers to purchase luxury products when they have limited opportunity to process brand information displayed by the advertisements (MacInnis & Jaworski 1989). Also, travelers may not respond to the advertisement because of limited education, product knowledge, and brand message. Distractions, time compression of the message, and the inability of the consumer to control the space in which the message is delivered could also lead to an indifferent attitude towards purchases. Travelers can also be easily distracted from the primary task of brand browsing and processing the information to the secondary task of talking, reducing the chances of impulse purchases.

An important difference between the traditional shopping experience and the airport environment is the waiting time. Travelers waiting for their flights may be bored, prompting them to wander around. So, the more time they spend on browsing, the more they learn about brands and their messages. The passenger's ability to mentally process advertising significantly increases after the security checkpoint, as they proceed to the gates through the main corridor. In fact, 60 percent of travelers walking in the last third of the concourse appeared to notice advertisements located in the corridor and near retail outlets (Wilson & Till 2008). Advertisement strategy at airports significantly differs from the regular shopping environment, as travelers experience fluctuating levels of stress while at airports. The most effective placement of advertisements in airports seems to be after the security checks when travelers' stress levels are reduced. Now they are in a place where they can browse more freely without the anxiety of missing their flights. Large airports also force travelers to arrive at their boarding gates as soon as possible, giving travelers more time to browse and buy (Crawford & Melewar 2003).

Luxury Retailing

Travel-related shopping can result in a unique frame of mind that can influence consumers to purchase high-involvement products (Perng, Chow, & Liao 2010). Depending upon the reasons for traveling, travelers may experience different emotions such as excitement, joy, reduced stress level, and social or emotional gratification that can trigger purchase intention (Hausman 2000). In this context, airport terminals are ideal venues for luxury retailing as travelers have the time and money to spend. Airport retailers now offer an impressive array of luxury products and services to meet the demand, such as *sustenance* (e.g. caviar, champagne, and a chef to cook), *shelter* (e.g. accommodation with spa bath and sun-bathing tower), *clothing* or *apparel* (e.g. sheepskin coats with accessories, perfume, and jewelry), and *leisure* (e.g. entertainment and sporting goods) (Berry 1994). Consumers are also willing to pay a high price for other premium goods such as home furnishings, fine arts, handmade crafts, and antiques (Swanson 2004). Unique duty-free products, wrapping, special design, and international brands make airport shopping more prestigious and desirable for luxury products. In fact, luxury products have become an important element in the travel and tourism industry, and an important source of revenue for many airports (Park, Reisinger, & Noh 2010). Hong Kong International Airport, for instance, carries more than 30 high-end designer clothing shops; Singapore Changi Airport offers cinemas, saunas, and a tropical butterfly forest, whereas Las Vegas's McCarran International Airport has a museum and Amsterdam Airport Schiphol has a Dutch Master's art gallery (Kasarda 2008). The increased interest in luxury products and services and customers' willingness to buy the luxury products lead airport retailers to feature duty-free shops, luxury brands, boutiques, and specialty retail and upscale restaurants, among others. Indeed, several factors can motivate travelers to buy luxury products, such as availability (e.g. exclusive, unique design; superb performance; superior substitute), convenience and quality shopping provided by the airports, and experimental motivations such as gift ideas, promotions, and courteous customer services (Lin & Chen 2013). Travelers seem to gravitate towards luxury products at the airport, because of the exotic stimuli of being in an out-of-home environment and to reduce the boredom that comes from being confined in the pre-boarding area before departure. Also, individuals who spend large amounts of time at airports, such as employees, might also be more likely to spend on products to satisfy utilitarian needs, such as food (Sulzmaier 2001).

Impulse Shoppers

Impulse buying relates to actions undertaken without a problem previously having been consciously recognized or a buying intention formed before entering the store (Engel & Blackwell 1982). Fashion-oriented impulse relates to purchases that are motivated by self-suggestion to buy the new fashion product without a previous experience. Fashion-oriented impulse purchases can be influenced by a shopper's own positive emotions (Mattila & Enz 2002). The general population tries to avoid impulse purchasing because it could be considered a social stigma. Studies indicate that only 20 percent of consumers feel guilty about making impulse purchases, whereas more than 40 percent feel good about making impulse purchases (Rook & Hoch 1985). In fact, impulse buying is a prevalent feature of shopper behavior in most retail settings, including airports (Hausman 2000; McGoldrick & Andre 1997). Gift buying is the dominant consumer behavior at the airport. Brand name products also provide passengers the satisfaction they need, aiding the impulse buying (Perng, Chow, & Liao 2010). As such, when travelers spend more time in airports, they are more likely to spend more (Torres, Dominquez, Valdes, & Aza 2005). Business travelers spend more time at airports than vacationers. Being on vacation increases the likelihood of purchasing because of positive perceptions of the retail environment (D'Alfonso, Jiang, & Wan 2013). Companions such as children often seem to stimulate unplanned purchases. Parents may feel obligated to honor the purchase requests made by their children. Airport retailers can enhance their store performance by understanding impulsive consumer behavior.

Apathetic Shoppers

Apathetic shoppers are individuals who do not spend much time and effort in shopping, have pessimistic views of retailers, and are unaffected by price resulting from a higher placement of value on convenience (Tatzel 1982). They are likely to engage in shopping that satisfies a utilitarian need or a planned goal-oriented purchase (Irani & Hanzaee 2011). These shoppers create value by not exerting effort in acquiring the product. Apathetic shoppers are less likely to trust retailers' tactics, special offers, or deals that can stimulate an impulse purchase. In fact, they have high self-control to curb the urge to shop impulsively. However, some airport retail settings may provide the ideal environment that could encourage them to behave differently. For example, apathetic consumers may enter a shop intending to make a planned purchase but might come across a product that triggers a reminder that they have another need to be satisfied, such as certain travel essentials or gifts and/or souvenirs for family, friends, or coworkers, while killing time (Kah & Lee 2014). Therefore, apathetic shoppers represent a unique challenge for airport retailers as they are the least likely to engage in impulse purchases. They also do not respond well to high-pressure sales tactics used by retailers. Therefore, airport retailers may earn the trust of apathetic buyers if they use a low-pressure method of selling (Kennedy, Ferrell, & LeClaire 2001).

Franchising

Most luxury brands originate from very few countries, with France, Italy, Switzerland, the UK, and the US accounting for the majority of global luxury sales. Although country of origin plays a significant role in a luxury brand's sales, they are generally global brands. The market for luxury goods continues to grow substantially globally because of economic expansion and growth in emerging markets (Shukla 2010). Economic factors such as an increase in the size of disposable income, a lower unemployment rate, and a growing number of wealthy consumers in emerging countries have also led to more favorable market conditions for luxury consumptions (Truong, McColl, & Kitchen 2009). Navigating the intricacies of the dynamic luxury industry to successfully manage a luxury brand is a complex process that requires more strategic than tactical decisions (Andal-Ancion, Coyle, & French 2010). Luxury products and services are equally in demand in both developed nations and emerging markets. However, entry mode differs from developed nations and emerging markets (Brown, Dev, & Zhou 2003).

For example, consumption of luxury goods appears to be about 20 percent annually in India (Tak & Pareek 2016). So, retail managers look for new market avenues for growth opportunities. One of the ways to expand business or enter a new market is through franchising.

Franchising Strategy

Franchising refers to an organizational form in which the owner of a protected trademark grants another person the right to operate under the trademark for production or distribution purposes. Franchising continues to be the fastest growing retail format for international expansion (White 2010). Luxury brands seek local investors to franchise brands and business models—marketing strategy and plan, operating manuals and standards, quality control, and a continuing process of assistance and guidance—for a fee and royalty. The relationship between the franchisor and the franchisee forms trust, resulting in greater openness, knowledge sharing, and appreciation for each partner's contribution to the success of the venture. As a result, franchise members do not believe that it is necessary to guard against the opportunistic behavior of their partner (Corsten & Kumar 2005). Some luxury brands—Prada, Hermès, Chanel, Ralph Lauren, Valentino, and Giorgio Armani, among others—have expanded through the franchising strategy. Indeed, partnering with a local franchisee gives the company access to the in-depth knowledge of the market and capabilities.

Franchising strategy is also used to mitigate inherent risks associated with foreign direct investments, high uncertainty, and lack of resources or knowledge of the new markets. Risks can be shared between franchisors and franchisees, while franchisors can benefit from the royalties paid by the franchisees. But because of the lack of control over operation and management of franchising, the franchisee may lack the incentive to keep up with the brand standards, which could lead to creating negative perceptions (Jin & Sternquist 2003). It is particularly important because luxury stores call for significant investments upfront, either in a standalone store or in a store in a mall. Many luxury brand retailers can capitalize on shopping malls that offer convenience, familiarity, cleanness, and security (Josiam, Kinley, & Kim 2005; Littrell, Paige, & Song 2004). As a franchisor, brands lose control to a certain extent, which can be risky to execute luxury brands' image in a new market. But in general, franchising strategy reduces the anxiety of both parties.

Franchising at Airports

International airports are excellent outlets for luxury brands. Their remarkably clean and air-conditioned environments resemble a luxury shopping mall. Shops at airports are beautifully lit and attract attention. The open floor plan and the doorless, democratic layout of the stores at airports give a sense of confidence and opportunity for travelers to enter who otherwise may feel intimidated by the ambience of a luxury store. Most international airports have luxury brand shops all in a row that are easy to reach and browse. The increased traffic of affluent customers at airports also provides opportunities for luxury brands to strengthen their brand awareness, increase recognition, and maximize sales potential on a global scale. Horizontal diversification by brands into other product categories (e.g. Bulgari, from a jewelry brand to cosmetics) and vertical diversification into different enterprises (e.g. Versace creating a relatively less expensive diffusion line such as Versus) appear to be a common strategy among French and Italian luxury brands (Seringhaus 2005). The shiny airports provide a range of shopping opportunities and experiences for travelers. Tiffany, Chanel, Hermès, Bulgari, Burberry, Chanel, and others are particularly noticeable at airports. Also, noticeable luxury brand franchisees include hotels. Other luxury brands in fashion, accessories, and jewelry sectors may consider the franchising agreement as a long-term exclusive agreement for a specified duration of time and territory, with a minimum agreed turnover and performance target. Some luxury brands may not charge a royalty fee or an annual fixed fee, limiting themselves to the revenues from sales only. Although *ordinary* brands may sign a franchising agreement without having agreed on location first, *luxury* brands usually sign an agreement once a desirable location is secured, making airport locations an ideal candidate for luxury brand franchisee outlets. Luxury airport retailing through franchising is an optimal mode of entry in emerging markets where the market is not developed enough to support premium category malls. Further, security is an added advantage, along with some tax incentives at airports. The franchisee option would reduce the financial risk by eliminating the need for high initial capital investments. Similarly, the franchise fees and royalties may be a secure and less volatile stream of revenue for franchisers in a market with uncertain conditions.

Flagship Luxury Stores

Flagship luxury stores are usually corporate-owned (i.e. not franchised) mono-brand stores whose objectives are to develop and build a brand rather than generate profit. So, a flagship store offers a full spectrum of products across categories such as men, women, accessories, and children, among others, and thus acts as a publicity vehicle for the brand to enhance its image, personality, and identity. To accommodate the wide spectrum of luxury goods and to showcase it, flagship stores can be five to eight times larger than the typical retail store. The stores may extend, on average, to four sales floors, as opposed to the norm of no more than two floors (Doherty 2009). To differentiate and maintain exclusivity, flagship stores are not only extra-large, but also have historic structure, architectural beauty, innovative fixtures, and unique décor that attract luxury fashion enthusiasts. Naturally, flagship stores make a statement about the brand, act as the most representative store, and serve as the primary point of entry into a new market. This mode of market entry is usually restricted to large capital cities on premium shopping streets—Bond Street, London; Fifth Avenue, New York; and Avenue Montaigne, Paris—where the store's widest and deepest product range can serve to showcase the brand's position, image, and values (Moore & Doyle 2010). Because of the grandeur of the flagship stores, their setup and operating costs are exorbitant. So, most luxury brands can sustain only a handful of flagship stores. Thus, having flagship stores means the company has reached a level of maturity such that the store can sustain its operation by sheer brand identity, visibility, desirability, and, of course, philosophy. Indeed, flagship stores are also tourist destinations and are often visited by non-traditional customers of the brand. Given the public relations nature and non-monetary objectives of flagship stores, the franchising option may be an inherently less effective strategy, which is based on royalty claims on gross revenue.

Corporate-Owned Luxury Stores

Corporate ownership refers to a system in which the head office has full control over the operation and management of a firm. Luxury corporate-owned stores are smaller versions of flagship stores that are used to enter a foreign country through foreign direct investment. The corporate model of foreign direct investment allows luxury brands to have complete control over the internal and external operations of the store such as pricing, promotion, marketing, reporting, and executive decisions. The high degree of control over foreign operations can (1) facilitate the implementation of global marketing strategies, which emphasize standardization, integration, and coordination; (2) protect luxury brands' specific advantages such as intellectual property rights; (3) improve store efficiency by aligning goal congruence; and (4) yield higher profits and returns (Anderson & Gatignon 1986). These corporate stores are preferable when resources are available in the foreign or local markets. But the high controlling costs may lead luxury brands to consider franchising as an alternative option (Ingham & Thompson 1994).

Pop-up Stores

Pop-up stores are very small and usually remain open for a short period of time at a particular location. The location of a pop-up store is determined by the same factors as any luxury flagship store. Both retail formats offer value in publicity through prime locations. Luxury brands such as Chanel and Hermès have opened pop-up stores in Paris, London, New York, and Tokyo. Usually, their locations are near the brand's parent store. Pop-up stores are also used to test marketing effectiveness, luxury product demand, and gravitational force of the locations, among others. Pop-up stores rely on viral or word-of-mouth marketing techniques, conveying the message that a temporary luxury store has been set up. It also creates events that attract the interests of the media and arouse consumer interests. So, pop-up stores do not incur heavy advertising costs. These stores often operate during public events, holidays, or new product launches. These stores are extremely effective in generating sales and rotating luxury products through extensive reporting of the events in the press and on the Internet. Rapid sales in a very short period of time occur, because the sales are restricted in time and space, making this approach very lucrative. These luxury pop-up stores also typically showcase one-off and limited editions of products to create a sense of urgency among shoppers. Indeed, these stores are an effective way for luxury brands to enter different retail areas with low risks, costs, and marketing, while being accessible to customers. Consumers find the pop-up stores very welcoming and easily accessible because the stores are less crowded and simpler in decoration, and products are displayed in a more attractive way (De Lassus & Freire 2014). Consumers experience a unique, immersive environment that engages them and generates a feeling of relevance and connection. Some other brands—Kate Spade, Gucci, Louis Vuitton, and Colette, among others—have also opened pop-up stores recently.

Luxury Services

Luxury services are difficult to define as they cover a wide variety of different and complex activities. In general, the term can refer to any activity that serves a need yet does not result in ownership even when paid. For example, renting, booking, or staying in a luxury five-star hotel may serve a physical or psychological need, but it does not extend to ownership of the room. The same concept applies to other service providers such as physicians, lawyers, and professors, among others. In the context of luxury travel and tourism, services can be divided into categories such as luxury resorts/hotels, private villas, luxury cruises, private islands, yacht rentals, adventure travel, luxury special-interest travel, private jet holidays, and tailor-made tours. Luxury hunting is also becoming popular in some countries in Africa. For example, in Botswana, which has the largest population of elephants (130,000), the government recently decided to sell seven hunting licenses at exorbitant prices, allowing hunters to kill ten elephants each in *controlled hunting areas* on the grounds that hunting would help the areas most impacted by the *human-wildlife conflict* (Maseko 2020). Luxury is not limited to human beings only. In the context of pets, China has a five-star dog hotel which offers a cinema, swimming pools, and luxury rooms for its four-legged (canine) guests (BBC 2018).

Recently, the traditional concept of staying at luxury five-star hotels and resorts has shifted to include a wide variety of exclusive and unique experiences such as unique dining, pampering spas, and custom-made experiential tours (Yesawitch 2006). Luxury travelers are also concerned about privacy. So, they are willing to pay a premium to have remote hotel suites, secluded tables at restaurants, private villas with a private beach or pool, personal tour guides, trainers, and gourmet chefs. It is interesting to note that during the COVID-19 pandemic in 2020, some hotels (e.g. Mövenpick) in Thailand saw an opportunity to offer luxury isolation packages as an alternative to the government-funded 14-day quarantine for returning travelers. Bangkok has five Thai government–approved hotels to provide packages for people who wish to self-fund a more premium isolation period (Taylor 2020).

There is a trend for luxury *product* brands to branch out in the high-quality luxury *service* sector. For example, Bulgari opened Bulgari Hotels and Resorts and Bulgari Hotel Yacht Club in Dubai, UAE. Quality of services can be measured on broad five broad dimensions (Parasuraman, Zeithaml, & Berry 1988): tangibles (appearance of physical elements), reliability (dependable and accurate performance), responsiveness (promptness and helpfulness), assurance (credibility, security, competence, and courtesy), and empathy (easy access, good communications, and customer understanding). Franchising of services is relatively easier and more profitable than manufacturing or other form of foreign direct investment. But it is more difficult to maintain (though required through franchisee contracts) quality of services on all dimensions at numerous franchisee locations around the world. As a result, services in a franchisee luxury hotel in emerging markets may not be identical to the same corporate-owned brand in the US, even if their infrastructure may look impressive externally. It is about impeccable service. Most luxury hotels are franchisees.

Conclusion

It is crucial for airport retailers to attract potential customers. A unique airport environment triggers excitement and social and emotional gratification, which is conducive to stimulating purchases of luxury products and services. Airports also provide an excellent opportunity for retailers to introduce their products to many customers from around the world who have different demographics and psychographics. Travelers usually feel relaxed after security checks. They are willing to spend time browsing stores and most likely engage in shopping behavior. As such, luxury products' unique design, exclusive packaging, durability, and superior quality attract customers from various cultures. However, airport retailers need to pay particular attention to apathetic shoppers who are least interested in browsing, shopping, or conforming to impulse purchasing.

Experiential Learning

1. Compare luxury stores (corporate-owned versus franchisees) and luxury products offered at different terminals (domestic versus international) of the same airport.

2. Visit www.thestorefront.com and find a suitable location and its rent to open a luxury pop-up store in your area. Develop a business plan for a pop-up store for a year. Show break-even points in terms of both revenue ($) and number of units (#). Assume any missing data with justification. Comment on the likelihood of achieving the break-even point under various scenarios (pessimistic, most likely, and optimistic).

3. List and discuss ten luxury services, such as hotels and swimming, offered at airports. www.cnn.com/travel/article/airport-swimming-pools/index.html

References

ACINA 2005. Airports council international North America. *Retail and Concessions*. www.aci-na.org/asp/subject.asp?page=122 [Accessed on July 2, 2020].

Andal-Ancion, A., Coyle, C. & French, L. 2010. Reacting to consumer trends, reaching new markets, and mitigating risks in a tough economic environment. *The Licensing Journal*, *30*(1), 1–7.

Anderson, E. & Gatignon, H. 1986. Mode of foreign entry: A transaction cost analysis and propositions. *Journal of International Business Studies*, *17*(Fall), 1–26.

Appold, S. & Kasarda, J. 2006. The appropriate scale of US airport retail activities. *Journal of Air Transport Management*, *12*(6), 277–287.

BBC. 2018. Pampered pooches: China's luxury hotel for dogs. www.bbc.com/news/av/world-asia-china-43054855/pampered-pooches-china-s-luxury-hotel-for-dogs [Accessed on July 2, 2020].

Berry, C. 1994. *The idea of luxury: A conceptual and historical investigation*. Cambridge: Cambridge University Press.

Bingman, C. 1996. Airports as retail malls? What are the criteria for a successful airport retail mall? 5th Airports Council International Conference, Marselle.

Brown, J.R., Dev, C.S. & Zhou, Z. 2003. Broadening the foreign market entry mode decision: Separating ownership and control. *Journal of International Business Studies*, *34*, 473–488.

Corsten, D. & Kumar, N. 2005. Do suppliers benefit from collaborative relationships with large retailers? An empirical investigation of efficient consumer response adoption. *Journal of Marketing*, *69*(3), 80–94.

Crawford, G. & Melewar, T.C. 2003. The importance of impulse purchasing behaviour in the international airport environment. *Journal of Consumer Behaviour*, *3*(1), 85–98.

D'Alfonso, T., Jiang, C. & Wan, Y. 2013. Airport pricing concession revenues and passenger types. *Journal of Transport Economics and Policy*, *47*(1), 71–89.

de Lassus, C. & Freire, N.A. 2014. Access to the luxury brand myth in pop-up stores: A netnographic and semiotic analysis. *Journal of Retailing and Consumer Services*, *21*(1), 61–68.

Dholakia, U. 2000. Temptation and resistance: An integrated model of consumption impulse formation and enactment. *Psychology & Marketing*, *17*(11), 955–982.

Doganis, R. 1992. *The airport business*. London: Routledge.

Doherty, A.M. 2009. Market and partner selection processes in international retail franchising. *Journal of Business Research*, *62*(5), 528–534.

Engel, J. & Blackwell, R. 1982. *Consumer behaviour*. New York: Holt, Reinehart and Winston.

Freathy, P. & O'Connell, F. 1999. Planning for profit: The commercialization of European airports. *Long Range Planning, 32*(2), 587–597.

Hausman, A. (2000). A multi-method investigation of consumer motivations in impulse buying behavior. *Journal of Consumer Marketing, 17*(5), 403–426.

Hsu, C. & Chao, C. 2005. Space allocation for commercial activities at international passenger terminals. *Logistics and Transportation Review, 41*(1), 29–51.

Ingham, H. & Thompson, S. 1994. Wholly-owned vs. collaborative ventures for diversifying financial services. *Strategic Management Journal, 15*(4), 325–334.

Irani, N. & Hanzaee, K.H. 2011. The effects of variety-seeking buying tendency and price sensitivity on utilitarian and hedonic value in apparel shopping satisfaction. *International Journal of Marketing Studies, 3*(3), 89.

Jin, B. & Sternquist, B. 2003. The influence of retail environment on price perceptions an exploratory study of US and Korean students. *International Marketing Review, 20*(6), 643–660.

Josiam, B., Kinley, T. & Kim, Y. 2005. Involvement and the tourist shopper: Using the involvement construct to segment the American tourist shopper at the mall. *Journal of Vacation Marketing, 11*(2), 135–154.

Kah, J. & Lee, S. 2014. Beyond adoption of travel technology: It's application to unplanned travel behaviours. *Journal of Travel & Tourism Marketing, 31*(6), 667–680.

Kasarda, J. 2008. Shopping in the airport city and metropolis. *Research Review, 15*(2), 50–56.

Kennedy, M.S., Ferrell, L. & LeClaire, D. 2001. Consumers' trust of salesperson and manufacturer: And empirical study. *Journal of Business Research, 51*(1), 73–86.

Lin, Y. & Chen, C. 2013. Passengers' shopping motivations and commercial activities at airports: The moderating effects of time pressure and impulse buying tendency. *Tourism Management, 36*, 426–434.

Littrell, M., Paige, R. & Song, K. 2004. Senior travelers: Tourism activities and shopping behaviours. *Journal of Vacation Marketing, 10*(4), 348–362.

Lloyd, J. 2003. Airport technology, travel, and consumption. *Space and Culture, 6*(2), 93–109.

MacInnis, D.J. & Jaworski, B.J. 1989. Information processing from advertisements: Toward an integrative framework. *The Journal of Marketing, 53*(Oct), 1–23.

Maseko, N. 2020. Botswana auctions off permits to hunt elephants. www.bbc.com/news/world-africa-51413420 [Accessed on July 2, 2020].

Mattila, A. & Enz, C. 2002. The role of emotions in service encounters. *Journal of Service Research, 4*(4), 268–277.

McGoldrick, P. & Andre, E. 1997. Consumer misbehavior: Promiscuity or loyalty in grocery shopping. *Journal of Retailing and Consumer Services, 4*(2), 73–81.

Moore, C.M. & Doyle, S.A. 2010. The evolution of a luxury brand: The case of Prada. *International Journal of Retail & Distribution Management, 38*(11), 915–927.

Morgan, N. & Pritchard, A. 2004. Meeting the destination branding challenge. In N. Morgan, A. Pritchard, & R. Pride (Eds.), *Destination branding* (pp. 59–79). Oxford: Elsevier.

Newman, S. & Lloyd-Jones, T. 1999. Airport and travel termini retailing: Strategies, trends and market dynamics. *Financial Times*, 1.

Omar, O. & Kent, A. 2001. International airport influences on impulsive shopping: Trait and normative approach. *International Journal of Retail & Distribution Management, 29*(5), 226–235.

Parasuraman, A., Zeithaml, V.A. & Berry, L. 1988. SERVQUAL: A multi item scale for measuring consumer perceptions of service quality. *Journal of Retailing*, 64(1), 12–40.

Park, K.S., Reisinger, Y. & Noh, E.H. 2010. Luxury shopping in tourism. *International Journal of Tourism Research*, 12(2), 164–178.

Perng, S., Chow, C. & Liao, W. 2010. Analysis of shopping preference and satisfaction with airport retailing products. *Journal of Air Transport Management*, 16(5), 279–283.

Piron, F. 1991. Defining impulse purchasing. *Advances in Consumer Research*, 18, 509–514.

Rook, D. & Hoch, S. 1985. Consuming impulses. *Advances in Consumer Research*, 12(1), 23–27.

Rowley, J. & Slack, F. 1999. The retail experience in airport departure lounges: Reaching for timelessness and placelessness. *International Marketing Review*, 16(4/5), 363–376.

Seringhaus, F.H.R. 2005. Selling luxury brands online. *Journal of Internet Commerce*, 4(1), 1–25.

Shukla, P. 2010. Status consumption in cross-national context: Socio-psychological, brand and situational antecedents. *International Marketing Review*, 27(1), 108–129.

Slater, S. & Olson, E. 2001. Marketing's contribution to the implementation of business strategy: An empirical analysis. *Strategic Management Journal*, 22(11), 1055–1067.

Stern, H. 1962. The significance of impulse buying today. *The Journal of Marketing*, 26(2), 59–62.

Sulzmaier, S. 2001. *Consumer-oriented business design: The case of airport management*. Germany: Physica-Verlag.

Swanson, K. 2004. Tourists' and retailers' perception of souvenirs. *Journal of Vacation Marketing*, 10(4), 363–377.

Tak, P. & Pareek, A. 2016. Consumer attitude towards luxury brands: An empirical study. *IUP Journal of Brand Management*, 13(1), 7–19.

Tatzel, M. 1982. Skill and motivation in clothes shopping: Fashion-conscious, independent, anxious, and apathetic consumers. *Journal of Retailing*, 58(4), 90–97.

Taylor, C. 2020. Thai hotels are offering luxury quarantine packages as an alternative to state-funded isolation. www.cnbc.com/2020/06/02/thai-hotels-are-offering-luxury-quarantine-packages.html [Accessed on July 2, 2020].

Thomas, D. 1997. Retail and leisure developments at London Gatwick. *Commercial Airport*, 38–41.

Torres, E., Dominquez, J.S., Valdes, L. & Aza, R. 2005. Passenger waiting time in an airport and expenditure carried out in the commercial areas. *Journal of Air Transport Management*, 11(6), 363–367.

Truong, Y., McColl, R. & Kitchen, P.J. 2009. New luxury brand positioning and the emergence of masstige brands. *Journal of Brand Management*, 16(5/6), 375–382.

Van Oel, C. & Van Den Berkhof, F.W. 2013. Consumer preferences in the design of airport passenger areas. *Journal of Environmental Psychology*, 36, 280–290.

White, D.W. 2010. The impact of marketing strategy creation style on the formation of a climate of trust in a retail franchise setting. *European Journal of Marketing*, 44(1), 162–179.

Wilson, R. & Till, B. 2008. Airport advertising effectiveness: An exploratory field study. *Journal of Advertising*, 37(1), 59–72.

Yesawitch, P.C. 2006. Portrait of affluent travelers. *Hotel Management*, November.

Yu, C. & Bastin, M. 2010. Hedonic shopping value and impulse buying behavior in transitional economies: A symbiosis in the mainland China marketplace. *Journal of Brand Management*, 18(2), 105–114.

5   Contemporary Marketing

Virtual Reality

Virtual reality (VR) is a sensory technology in which the viewer is immersed in a complex symbolic universe, which allows for a virtual experiential marketing experience through the psychological sensation of the presence achieved through the immersion (Marini 2012; Shaev 2013; Winn 1995). In VR, audio and video signals, produced by a computer program, are essentially signs and symbols with which the viewer interacts. The signified ideas form meaning in the mind of a viewer or interpreter (Belanger 2009). Viewers are immersed in the environment and influenced by the atmospherics, which leads to an emotional reaction of pleasure, acceptance, satisfaction, and overall positive attitude (Hoffman & Turley 2002). The richness of the medium depends on its capacity for immediate feedback, the number of cues available, language variety, and personalization. All these attributes can be programmed and provided in a virtual environment, which makes VR a powerful marketing platform (Daft, Lengel, & Trevino 1987). Advances in devices and programs with interface technologies have made the possibility of three-dimensional (3D) creations of bodily structures for viewing and interactions in a 3D virtual environment possible (Nguyen & Wilson 2009). Because of the interactivity and immersion capabilities of VR technology, viewers feel like they are physically a part of an experience or environment, which creates the same feelings and cognitions that arise from being in the real world. Further, VR technology allows consumers to visualize themselves in the product and evoke psychological identification and affective emotional ties to the product (Liang & Wang 2008). So, well-designed experience creates favorable moods, behaviors, and emotional attachments, which lead to strong beliefs and attitudes towards products, and therefore brand image (Klein 2003; McCole 2004). A carefully designed narrative and properly coded VR environment signifies to consumers the notion that they are present in a luxury environment such as an exclusive fashion show. This kind of experience was previously only attainable by those in a given geographical location or those with a certain status, but VR technology now allows for expanding geographical reach, creating emotional attachment to the brand, and increasing purchase intention through virtual experiential marketing of luxury products and services. To achieve success, an experience should include personal relevance, novelty, surprise, learning, and engagement—all of which are possible through VR technology in simulated environments (Poulsson & Kale 2004). Luxury brands such as Tommy Hilfiger, Yves Saint Laurent, and Christian Dior use VR technology to offer customers a virtual shopping experience. Thirty million VR technology–based headsets are estimated to be sold globally by 2020 (Wheeler 2016). Indeed, VR technology gives participants experiences as opposed to just information.

Online Marketing

It was thought for years that advertising luxury products was not necessary to increase sales (Freire 2014). The development of online technologies offers new communication tools for brands to communicate and increase brand visibility to the general public (Geerts & Veg-Sala 2011). Given that luxury brands heavily emphasize the importance of a sensory experience, one may wonder how long the online business model can last, because of its inability to come in contact physically with products and salespeople (Pine & Gilmore 1999). Some marketers of luxury brands are reluctant to go online as contradictions are apparent between the online world and luxury perception (Muller, Kocher, & Ivens 2007). Luxury relies on exclusivity and the perceived image of its consumers that only a very few can access it. If anybody can access the luxury brand online, then such exclusivity may disappear and degrade the perception of luxury itself. Online marketing may push luxury products very fast to potential consumers (Chandon, Laurent, & Valette-Florence 2016). There is also an apparent risk of loss of image control and thus loss of prestige value (de Chernatony 2001). The evolution of online marketing techniques and its innovative nature may leave some marketers skeptical, but it is now being accepted as part of any comprehensive marketing strategy (Okonkwo 2009). So, luxury brands have a love-hate relationship with online marketing. Burberry embraces online marketing, whereas Prada may be cautious. The Internet is now part of consumers' daily lives. Luxury marketers need to adapt to the technology and remain competitive in the industry. Scholars also advocate for online marketing for luxury products and services.

Social Media

The term *social media* refers to a group of Internet-based applications (e.g. Facebook, Twitter, Instagram, etc.) that build on the ideological and technological foundations of the Web. It allows the creation and exchange of *user-generated content* (Kaplan & Haenlein 2010). Social media is a relatively new marketing channel that has created a new platform for brands to reach, target, and engage consumers (Gallaugher & Ransbotham 2010; Kozinets, de Valck, Wojnicki, & Wilner 2010) while building long-term relationships (Zhu & Chen 2015) and communicating brand messages (Okonkwo 2009).

Luxury brands are able to engage in meaningful and reciprocal interactions with customers in ways that were not previously possible with traditional one-way advertising mediums such as television, radio, and print. Social media websites have changed the way brand content is created, distributed, and consumed by transferring the power to shape brand images from marketers to the consumers' online connection, content, and community. Luxury brands may use social media and play a leading role similar to websites and apps. The growing prevalence and popularity of social media has drastically changed the way firms communicate key messages to consumers— that is, shifting the relationship from a one-way dialogue to a two-way, reciprocal conversation. Although many luxury and fashion brands have been initially reluctant to utilize social media as a marketing tool, more and more luxury fashion retailers are embracing the digital revolution. Brands such as Burberry, DKNY, and Calvin Klein are now at the forefront of this movement, giving consumers unprecedented access to their brands (Kontu & Vecchi 2014).

Cost Effectiveness

The traditional media of advertisements—fashion shows, billboards, magazines, and television—are outdated and expensive. Print media, which is still used by many luxury brands, particularly fashion, is disappearing because of a low number of subscribers. However, social media can be a cost-effective and efficient tool for building brand image as it can reach more than two thirds of all Internet users (Correa, Hinsley, & De Zúñiga 2010; Spillecke & Perrey 2012). Specifically, it is an effective marketing tool for fashion brands to reach the youth segment. The majority of social media users are under age 35, making up 40–50 percent of the user base (Reisinger 2015). Twitter alone is made up of a whopping 90 percent of users under 30 years old in the UK (Sloan, Morgan, Burnap, & Williams 2015). Further, Twitter is a rich medium that can provide content with sight, sound, motion, interaction, and feedback (Kamal, Chu, & Pedram 2013). Some luxury and fashion brands have started using various social media—Facebook, Twitter, YouTube, and Instagram—to gain competitive advantage and persuade consumers (Schwedt, Chevalier, & Gutsatz 2012). Social media has a worldwide reach, so enormous potential to influence consumer behavior.

Trust

Social media marketing promotes higher consumer trust than traditional media marketing because of interaction among end users (Chaturvedi, Gupta, & Hada 2016). Through the interactions, consumers can comment and give their opinions in *real time* on available products online. Consumer trust is further established through interactions with other online users. Consumers believe social media is a trustworthy source of information (Mangold & Faulds 2009). Further, the social media engagement between fashion brands and shoppers can lead to increased consumer *believability* of marketing messages. The elevated believability often results in a positive marketing outcome for luxury brands, including increased purchase intention, customer equity, brand awareness, and decreased purchase risk perception (Chae & Ko 2016; Park & Kim 2015). By facilitating relationships between customers and brands in a free and entertaining online environment, luxury brands can create added value for their brands that can increase purchase intention among these consumers (Kim & Ko 2010).

Status

Consumers purchase luxury products for hedonistic or materialistic reasons, pleasure, or to express their social status, success, and group membership (Kapferer 1998). It is the group membership that makes social media a powerful marketing tool. Consumers make comparisons between their actual self and idealized media images as well as compare themselves to their aspirational and reference groups. As a result, social media becomes an effective platform where material possessions and consumption styles can be shared online among users (Lehdonvirta 2010). Consumers frequently turn to various types of social media for reviews and product information, because they perceive it as more trustworthy than corporate-sponsored communications (Mangold & Faulds 2009). Consumers make brand choices. But social media can confirm a choice, because it is used as a main product research channel. The use of social media enables brands to capitalize on emotional connections and influence consumers' purchasing decisions about status-enhancing luxury goods (Costa & Handley 2011).

Brand Equity

Social media positively affects increasing brand awareness and equity (Bruhn, Schoenmueller, & Schafer 2012). Potential customers have greater access to brand information in real time when they want it. The information can be presented in ways that can be easily processed and sorted through visual social media applications such as Pinterest and other sites that allow comparisons across a range of products. Many young and tech-savvy consumers are more likely to rely on and seek out product information from social media than from traditional advertising sources. This increased responsiveness to customer inquiries generates positive reactions to the brand, and in turn, bolsters customer equity (Chae & Ko 2016). Once consumers establish relationships with luxury or fashion brands through online information and social media interactions, they often exhibit an increased loyalty intention towards the brand (Park & Kim 2015). Luxury brands can use social media to communicate brand identity and build brand image in order to increase loyalty, willingness to pay a premium price, and future purchasing intentions (Kim & Ko 2012).

Visual Capability

Visual social media platforms such as Instagram and YouTube have become increasingly important for the fashion industry, which relies on aesthetics and visual representations (Workman & Caldwell 2007). These platforms also allow fashion brands to develop creative advertisements that might not be possible in a traditional format such as print. For example, consumers increasingly have better cameras on their phones, which feature higher-resolution screens that allow for more information on product craftsmanship to be visible. So, there are more opportunities for marketers to communicate and strengthen the brand image. Also, the capability for reciprocal communications allows brands to know more about their customers and offer innovative products and services for the segment. In emerging markets, consumers may not be able to buy monthly print publications, but they may have social media accounts at reasonable costs. This explains how powerful and effective social media can be in reaching remote markets. There is also a sense of realism and genuineness in social media marketing, because it is often accompanied by contents generated by actual people or events. The visual capability of social media presents valuable opportunities for luxury fashion brands to display their apparel in settings in which people pay attention to what others are wearing. When a brand is precisely and successfully marketed through social media, consumers of the target segment may desire it. Although social media provides new opportunities and benefits for managing the brand, it may be difficult (although possible) to measure the impact of social media marketing on brand success (Godey, Manthiou, Pederzoli, Rokka, Aiello, Donvito, & Singh 2016).

Mobile Marketing

Mobile marketing targets customers through mobile devices and the Internet. Different kinds of mobile marketing techniques exist—app-based websites, in-game, quick response (QR) code, location-based, and short messages service (SMS), among others. App-based mobile marketing involves ads popping up when an app is engaged, whereas in-game mobile marketing refers to mobile ads that appear within mobile games. QR codes are scanned by a user with their cameras to open the corresponding website. QR codes are frequently used in mobile marketing. Location-based mobile marketing ads appear on mobile devices based upon a person's location or business, whereas SMS involves sending ad information relating to deals or coupon codes to users via text messages on their mobile devices, so they can take advantage of the promotions quickly. Consumers spend significant amounts of time on app-based activities on their smartphones, which makes mobile marketing effective in approach and reach. The unique aspects of mobile marketing have enabled developing countries and emerging markets, which once lacked understanding of the technology, to rapidly approach parity with consumers in more developed countries (Ahanonu, Biggerstaff, Flacuks, & Hatfeild 2013).

Smartphone Era

About one third of US adults own smartphones (Rosenkrans & Myers 2012). Development of mobile applications has created possibilities to establish relationships with consumers. For luxury brands, the quality of their applications should reflect the high quality of their products. By personalizing their mobile marketing platforms, luxury brands can customize and express their uniqueness to build brand affinity and loyalty (Martin & Todorov 2010). Mobile devices and applications offer brands the opportunity to use a new channel to reach consumers and combine information search with consumer interaction (Ström, Vendel, & Bredican 2014). Because a mobile device or smartphone is a constant companion to a consumer, this supplementary channel can be used to create a relationship between the consumers and brands. The ambience that a brand creates on its app is related to the brand image, navigation, functionality, and interactivity (Hennigs, Wiedmann, & Klarmann 2012). From researching products to conducting transactions, to sharing a product review with their social network, people rely on their mobile devices to access advice to make the right decisions (Vlad 2011). Luxury brands may use mobile marketing as an informational tool and not necessarily as a selling tool, because luxury shoppers may need extended periods of time to make decisions.

Brand Extension

Extending a brand with a different identity (e.g. name, logo, etc.) from the parent brand is a marketing strategy. The absence of the *exclusivity* factor makes extended brands more accessible to a larger market. Armani has experimented and seen success in extending its brand to offer products ranging from books, furniture, and chocolates, to restaurants, bars, and spas (Albrecht, Backhaus, Gurzki, & Woisetschlager 2013). Because these brands are seen as separate from the original brand identity, mobile marketing can be effective in the marketing of such premium products without affecting the exclusivity of the original luxury brand too much. Luxury brands usually extend themselves into sectors beyond their core business. Established luxury brands may introduce new products (premium in nature) or services that provide growth opportunities (Aaker & Keller 1990). The new premium products have the advantage of using the brand association from the parent brand and therefore reduce overall costs of marketing campaigns. To be more accessible, premium brands may embrace social media, launch websites, and create a spectrum of products whose details and craftsmanship can be displayed on mobile applications for mass marketing. With the introduction of extended premium brands, these relatively less expensive and less marketing-intensive brands may pave the way for globalization. The new brand extension can create a new market overseas. By utilizing mobile marketing, premium brands can create a sense of desirability for their products to a wide range of potential customers.

However, the dominant driver of brand extension success for luxury and premium brands is overall extension fit and the consumer's involvement in the extension category (Albrecht, Backhaus, Gurzki, & Woisetschlager 2013). An unsuccessful brand extension may damage the parent brand's image and exclusivity. As such, luxury brands are sensitive to inconsistent brand cues, and thus the brand extensions need to remain consistent in terms of cues such as superior quality and high price (Hagtvedt & Patrick 2009). A consistent brand extension that incorporates the country's culture and norms may help the brand to be more relatable to the new market. Brands such as Nike golf clothing and Oakley shoes have successfully extended their brands from Nike shoes and Oakley glasses, respectively. GAP and Banana Republic are other successful examples. Despite extended brands having their own identity, they are still associated with the parent brand and thus reduce the costs of overall marketing.

Challenges

With the arrival of smartphone technology and the release of the iPhone in 2007, a very close interaction between consumers and mobile technology was established (Watson, McCarthy, & Rowley 2013). The technology and high-resolution screens may allow luxury brands to create an aesthetically pleasing application that can communicate its beauty and magic to the shopper. It may still be hard to communicate the value on a mobile application, because of the lack of physical connection with the product that the consumer requires to make a luxury purchase (Kapferer 1997). Further, the loss of exclusivity of luxury brands is the main concern for using mobile marketing, even though it has the potential to reach out to their target segment and grow brand loyalty. Although mobile marketing may be effective in promoting premium brands such as H&M, Forever21, etc., it may be ineffective for luxury brands such as Versace, Louis Vuitton, etc., that target wealthier, status-oriented customers for whom exclusivity is paramount. The aspect of exclusivity is a key characteristic of luxury products. Limited accessibility and rarity justify their exorbitant prices (Hennigs, Wiedmann, & Klarmann 2012). Exclusivity elements—specific store locations, excellent product presentation, skilled sales personnel, or multi-sensory experiences such as touch and smell that appeal to consumers' emotions—that can be maintained in a physical store may be difficult to portray on mobile applications. Given that luxury products are so desirable—the counterfeit luxury industry being four times the genuine luxury industry—it can be anticipated that the exclusivity trait of luxury may not subside, regardless of the use of mobile marketing, because the positive emotional benefits of luxury products will always lure customers, particularly first-time buyers of luxury items. Last but not least, some consumers may have a negative attitude towards mobile marketing because of the annoyance and invasion of privacy.

Celebrity Endorsement

Celebrity endorsements are used to create an aspirational brand image and to stimulate interest in the brand. They are usually not used as a marketing tool to sell products on a short-term basis, because luxury brands focus on status, prestige, and heritage appeals for long-term success. Even if celebrity endorsements are used to increase brand awareness, the focus is still on exclusivity by limiting the availability of luxury products. The most common products for celebrity endorsements appear to be perfumes and clothing. Celebrities can also have contracts with manufacturers to sell their products. To the viewer or potential consumer, it may be hard to discern whether a celebrity is a direct or indirect endorser—that is, whether they are contractually obligated to promote a brand or whether they do so on their own. Congruence between endorser and brand image is important. In an example of a negative indirect endorsement, Burberry's baseball caps were frequently being worn by football hooligans in England. This new trend led Burberry to stop production of the baseball caps and pay an undisclosed amount of money to a public figure to stop wearing their merchandise (Radón 2012). Celebrities wearing a particular brand can be seen by thousands within minutes as a result of the Internet.

Endorsements

Brands select celebrity endorsers for their products if they have a specific tie to the product or to the target audience so that their target audience is receptive to the advertisements, resulting in a higher rate of intent to purchase (Chang & Ko 2016). Louis Vuitton is strategically endorsed by celebrities—Jennifer Lopez and Uma Thurman, for example. In many instances, celebrity-endorsed versions of products are added to a product line to command a very high price. The new modified product line usually has the same recognizable style and quality of the luxury brand but features the endorser's name. The new line may be considered a premium or exclusive adaptation of the product because of its exclusiveness and endorsement by an aspirational figure. Nike's endorsement strategy resulted in a new line of products, specifically, Air Jordan, featuring higher prices and Michael Jordan's name; the new line generated high profits for the company (Keel & Nataraajan 2012). In another example, Hermès' Birkin and Kelly handbags are ultimate luxury product lines based on celebrity endorsements. Indeed, premiums can be charged above the regular price of the product if it is an exclusive line that was created with the celebrity. Although advertisements being endorsed by celebrities may be effective for luxury brands, true luxury brands such as Maybach cars, Brioni suits, and Harry Winston custom jewelry may not require celebrity endorsements because their brands speak for themselves. These are old, established luxury brands—a high status symbol.

Endorsement Effects

Celebrity endorsements usually increase brand sales substantially. In a study of firms that took part in celebrity endorsements, recorded gains of about a half percent on their returns were realized (Agrawal & Wagner 1995). In fact, the market, on average, anticipates the net discounted cash flow to be close to zero, implying that the benefits of a celebrity endorsement match their costs (Ding, Molchanov, & Stork 2011). However, celebrity endorsement may result in lower cash flow expectations if celebrities are perceived to be involved in undesirable events (Keel & Nataraajan 2012). Studies indicate that share price would decrease by about 3 percent if a negative event occurred involving a celebrity endorser (Carrillat, d'Astous, & Christianis 2014). So, the higher or lower perceived level of involvement of a celebrity endorser in an event will increase or decrease the stock return for the company that used them (Louie, Kulik, & Jacobson 2001). A tradeoff exists for luxury brands between achieving the objective of short-term, large-scale promotions through celebrity endorsements and maintaining exclusivity by non-endorsement that will result in long-term prestige and heritage.

Celebrity Reputation

The reputation of a celebrity endorser significantly impacts brand image. There is a risk that the endorser might engage in undesirable behavior—drug use or infidelity—that may damage both the reputation of the celebrity and the brand. For example, in 2009 Tiger Woods was embroiled in an adultery scandal; just two weeks after the news broke out, the firms he had endorsed, such as Nike, EA Sports, and PepsiCo, among others, lost returns on their investments. Luxury brand Tag Heuer also ended its endorsement relations with Woods in 2011. (However, Rolex partnered with Woods subsequently, suggesting that short-term financial losses could be rectified if the celebrity's image begins to recover.) As such, celebrity endorsers may also lose their likability over time. Celebrity likeability is not universal, either.

No Endorsement Strategy

Celebrity endorsement may be seen as seeking the celebrity's status and admitting that the luxury brand cannot sustain on its own. For a luxury brand, a well-preserved image and perception of luxury significantly contribute to the prestige factor of a product, which should be paramount over short-term financial results and increased sales through the endorsements (Kapferer & Bastien 2009). Collaborating with an endorser may also dilute the core aspects of a traditional luxury brand. For instance, rap artists have been known to promote luxury goods through their image and their lyrics, resulting in a short-term increase in sales for these products but a negative impact on long-term brand equity (Roberts 2002). Further, it may be difficult for a luxury brand to find a worldwide celebrity for its global consumers. American celebrities' endorsements may be extremely effective and appeal to consumers in the US but may fail to get the admiration of other global consumers. Because of the global nature of many luxury brands, celebrity endorsement may not be effective in a standardized campaign, unless the celebrity chosen is recognized and admired worldwide. Celebrities may appeal to the masses but fail to resonate with the target market that luxury brands are trying to reach. Another issue with celebrity endorsement is to find one whose influence is larger than the luxury brand itself. Otherwise, it would in fact cheapen the luxury brand image. Yet another concern is that some celebrities sign too many endorsement contracts at the same time, which dilutes the effects on all brands endorsed by that celebrity.

Semiotic Communications

The term *semiotics* relates to the use of signs and symbols for communications. The roots of semiotics trail back to at least as far as the pre-Socratic era, in which Hippocrates identified bodily manifested signs or symptoms or symbols (signifier) as conveyors of messages (signified). It was not until the turn of the 20th century that semiotics achieved its identity through the independently developed works of the Swiss linguist Ferdinand de Saussure and the American philosopher Charles Sanders Peirce (Sebeok 1976). It appears that creation and production of meaning in a message in a culture via communication is inherently natural. So, it may easily mean various things to various people, depending on how they take it (Olbertová 2014). It is argued that what we learn is not the *world*, but particular codes that are structured in society, so we can *share* our experiences of it (Deely 1982). Based on Saussure theory, sign or signifier can be simplified in three components: symbol, icon, and index. Communications managers use the semiotic components to design (e.g. logo, color, etc.) and convey intended messages to target audiences. In case of *symbol-based* communication, signifier is an arbitrary symbol with a meaning attached to it. For example, McDonalds' golden arches are arbitrary symbols (logos) but can signify food, burgers, America, etc. However, in the *icon-based mode* of communications, signifier is perceived as resembling the signified; for example, icons such as the *Mona Lisa* and Mahatma Gandhi evoke certain feelings. The *index-based* mode of communications is a causal relationship between signifier and signified. The Jaguar logo may signify speed, or the Lamborghini bull may indicate aggressiveness. Some luxury brands use subtle indexed logos. Cognitive efforts are required on the part of consumers to decipher their meaning.

Conclusion

The purpose of the chapter was to discuss contemporary marketing tools in five areas: virtual reality; online marketing; social media (i.e. cost effectiveness, trust, status, brand equity, and visual capability); mobile marketing (i.e. smartphones, brand extension, and the challenges); and celebrity endorsement (i.e. endorsement effects, celebrity reputation, and no endorsement strategy). Semiotic communications and its components were also defined and discussed in terms of creating meaning for luxury brands through logos.

Experiential Learning

1. Identify ten top luxury brands in your choice of industry that use the following marketing tools:

   a. Virtual reality devices
   b. Online presence
   c. Social media
   d. Celebrity endorsement

2. Identity 30 luxury logos/brands and classify them with justification in one of the following categories:

   a. Symbol
   b. Icon
   c. Index

   For a database of logos, visit: www.1000logos.net

3. Identify ten *luxury brands* that have *brand extensions* in the premium (relatively cheaper than luxury) category. Compare marketing strategies between both sets of brands (luxury versus premium). Select your marketing-based comparative indicators with justification.

References

Aaker, D.A. & Keller, K.L. 1990. Consumer evaluations of brand extensions. *Journal of Marketing*, 54(1), 27.

Agrawal, J. & Wagner, K. 1995. The economic worth of celebrity endorsers: An event study analysis. *Journal of Marketing*, 59(3), 56.

Ahanonu, K., Biggerstaff, P., Flacuks, A. & Hatfeild, M. 2013. Mobile brand interaction in Southeast Asia: A comparative study. *International Journal of Mobile Marketing*, 8(2), 5–18.

Albrecht, C.M., Backhaus, C., Gurzki, H. & Woisetschlager, D.M. 2013. Drivers of brand extension success: What really matters for luxury brands? *Psychology & Marketing*, 30(8), 647–659.

Belanger, W. 2009. A semiotic analysis of virtual reality. The Faculty of the Humanities Program in Candidacy for the Degree of Doctor Philosophy, 9.

Bruhn, M., Schoenmueller, V. & Schafer, D.B. 2012. Are social media replacing traditional media in terms of brand equity creation? *Management Research Review*, 35(9), 770–790.

Carrillat, F., d'Astous, A. & Christianis, H. 2014. Guilty by association: The perils of celebrity endorsement for endorsed brands and their direct competitors. *Psychology & Marketing, 31*(11), 1024–1039.

Chae, H. & Ko, E. (2016). Customer social participation in the social networking services and its impact upon the customer equity of global fashion brands. *Journal of Business Research, 69*(9), 3804–3812.

Chandon, J.L., Laurent, G. & Valette-Florence, P. 2016. Pursuing the concept of luxury: Introduction to the *Journal of Business Research* special issue on 'luxury marketing from tradition to innovation'. *Journal of Business Research, 69*, 299–303.

Chang, Y., & Ko, Y.J. 2016. Reconsidering the role of fit in celebrity endorsement: Associative-propositional evaluation (ape) accounts of endorsement effectiveness. *Psychology & Marketing, 33*(9), 678–691.

Chaturvedi, S., Gupta, S. & Hada, D.S. (2016). Perceived risk, trust and information seeking behavior as antecedents of online apparel buying behavior in India: An exploratory study in context of Rajasthan. *International Review of Management and Marketing, 6*(4), 935–943.

Correa, T., Hinsley, A.W. & De Zúñiga, H.G. 2010. Who interacts on the web? The intersection of users' personality and social media use. *Computers in Human Behavior, 26*(2), 247–253.

Costa, M. & Handley, L. 2011. Luxury brands: Removing exclusive tags risks permanent damage. *Marketing Week*, 16–21.

Daft, R.L., Lengel, R.H. & Trevino, L.K. 1987. Message equivocality, media selection, and manager performance: Implications for information systems. *MIS Quarterly, 11*(3), 355–366.

de Chernatony, L. 2001. Succeeding with brands on the Internet. *The Journal of Brand Management, 8*, 186–195.

Deely, J. 1982. *The pursuit of signs*. Bloomington: Indiana University Press.

Ding, H., Molchanov, A.E. & Stork, P.A. 2011. The value of celebrity endorsements: A stock market perspective. *Marketing Letters, 22*(2), 147–163.

Freire, N.A. 2014. When luxury advertising adds the identitary values of luxury: A semiotic analysis. *Journal of Business Research, 67*(12), 2666.

Gallaugher, J. & Ransbotham, S. 2010. Social media and customer dialog management at Starbucks. *MIS Quarterly Executive, 9*(4), 197–212.

Geerts, A. & Veg-Sala, N. 2011. Evidence on Internet communication management strategies for luxury brands. *Global Journal of Business Research, 5*, 81–94.

Godey, B., Manthiou, A., Pederzoli, D., Rokka, J., Aiello, G., Donvito, R. & Singh, R. 2016. Social media marketing efforts of luxury brands: Influence on brand equity and consumer behavior. *Journal of Business Research, 69*(12), 5833–5841.

Hagtvedt, H. & Patrick, V.M. 2009. The broad embrace of luxury: Hedonic potential as a driver of brand extendibility. *Journal of Consumer Psychology, 19*(4), 608–618.

Hennigs, N., Wiedmann, K.P., & Klarmann, C. 2012. Luxury brands in the digital age: Exclusivity versus ubiquity. *Marketing Review St. Gallen, 29*(1), 30–35.

Hoffman, D.L. & Turley, L.W. 2002. Atmospherics, service encounters and consumer decision making: An integrative perspective. *Journal of Marketing Theory and Practice, 10*(3), 33–47.

Kamal, S., Chu, S. & Pedram, M. 2013. Materialism, attitudes, and social media usage and their impact on purchase intention of luxury fashion goods among American and Arab young generations. *Journal of Interactive Advertising, 13*(1), 27–40.

Kapferer, J.N. 1997. Managing luxury brands. *Journal of Brand Management, 4*(4), 251–259.

Kapferer, J.N. 1998. Why are we seduced by luxury brands? *Journal of Brand Management*, 6(1), 44–49.

Kapferer, J.N. & Bastien, V. 2009. *The luxury strategy*. London: Kogan.

Kaplan, A.M. & Haenlein, M. (2010). Users of the world, unite! The challenges and opportunities of social media. *Business Horizons*, 53(1), 59–68.

Keel, A. & Nataraajan, R. 2012. Celebrity endorsements and beyond: New avenues for celebrity branding. *Psychology & Marketing*, 29(9), 690–703.

Kim, A.J. & Ko, E. 2010. Impacts of luxury fashion brand's social media marketing on customer relationship and purchase intention. *Journal of Global Fashion Marketing*, 1(3), 164–171.

Kim, A.J. & Ko, E. 2012. Do social media marketing activities enhance customer equity? An empirical study of luxury fashion brand. *Journal of Business Research*, 65, 1480–1486.

Klein, L.R. 2003. Creating virtual product experiences: The role of telepresence. *Journal of Interactive Marketing*, 17(1), 41–55.

Kontu, H. & Vecchi, A. (2014). Why all that noise: Assessing the strategic value of social media for fashion brands. *Journal of Global Fashion Marketing*, 5(3), 235–250.

Kozinets, R.V., de Valck, K., Wojnicki, A.C. & Wilner, S. 2010. Networked narratives: Understanding word-of-mouth marketing in online communities. *Journal of Marketing*, 74, 71–89.

Lehdonvirta, V. 2010. Online spaces have material culture: Goodbye to digital post-materialism and hello to virtual consumption. *Media, Culture, and Society*, 32(6), 883–889.

Liang, C.J. & Wang, W.H. 2008. Do loyal and more involved customers reciprocate retailer's relationship efforts? *Journal of Services Research*, 8(1), 63–90.

Louie, T.A., Kulik, R.L. & Jacobson, R. 2001. When bad things happen to the endorsers of good products. *Marketing Letters*, 12(1), 13–23.

Mangold, W.G. & Faulds, D.J. 2009. Social media: The new hybrid element of the promotion mix. *Business Horizons*, 52(4), 357–365.

Marini, D. 2012. Virtual reality as a communication process. *Virtual Reality*, 16(3), 233–241.

Martin, K. & Todorov, I. 2010. How will digital platforms be harnessed in 2010, and how will they change the way people interact with brands? *Journal of Interactive Advertising*, 10(2), 61–66.

McCole, P. 2004. Refocusing marketing to reflect practice: The changing role of marketing for business. *Marketing Intelligence and Planning*, 22(5), 531–539.

Muller, B., Kocher, B. & Ivens, B. 2007. Internet: La face cachée des produits de luxe. www.researchgate.net/profile/Brigitte_Mueller2/publication/228785756_Internet_la_face_cachee_des_produits_de_luxe/links/004635232feef5d7fa000000.pdf [Accessed on July 2, 2020].

Nguyen, N. & Wilson, T.D. 2009. A head in virtual reality: Development of a dynamic head and neck model. *Analytical Science Education*, 2, 294–301.

Okonkwo, U. 2009. Sustaining the luxury brand on the Internet. *Journal of Brand Management*, 16, 302–310.

Olbertová, M. 2014. Everything you always wanted to know about semiotics. *RW Connect*.

Park, H. & Kim, Y. (2015). Can a fashion brand be social?: The role of benefits of brand community within social network sites. *Journal of Global Fashion Marketing*, 6(2), 75–86.

Pine II, B.J. & Gilmore, J.H. 1999. *The experience economy: Work is theatre and every business a stage: Goods and services are no longer enough*. Boston: Harvard Business Press.

Poulsson, S.H.G. & Kale, S.H. 2004. The experience economy and commercial experiences. *The Marketing Review, 4*(3), 267–277.

Radón, A. 2012. Unintended brand endorsers' impact on luxury brand image. *International Journal of Marketing Studies, 4*, 110–113.

Reisinger, D. 2015. Millennials snapping up Snapchat, study finds. *CNET*. www.cnet.com/news/snapchat-a-magnet-for-youngsters-new-study-shows [Accessed on July 2, 2020].

Roberts, J. 2002. The rap of luxury. *Newsweek*. www.newsweek.com/rap-luxury-144731 [Accessed on July 2, 2020].

Rosenkrans, G. & Myers, K. 2012. Mobile advertising effectiveness. *International Journal of Mobile Marketing, 7*(3), 5–24.

Schwedt, G., Chevalier, M. & Gutsatz, M. 2012. *Luxury retail management: How the world's top brands provide quality product and service support*. Hoboken: Wiley.

Sebeok, T.A. 1976. *Contributions to the doctrine of signs*. Bloomington: Indiana University Press.

Shaev, Y. 2013. Virtual reality: The effects and phenomenon of sign. *Procedia-Social and Behavioral Sciences, 92*, 860–862.

Sloan, L., Morgan, J. & Burnap, P. & Williams, M. 2015. Who tweets? Deriving the demographic characteristics of age, occupation and social class from twitter user meta-data. *PLoS One, 10*(3), 1–20.

Spillecke, D. & Perrey, J. 2012. *Retail marketing and branding: A definitive guide to maximizing ROI*. Somerset: Wiley.

Ström, R., Vendel, M. & Bredican, J. 2014. Mobile marketing: A literature review on its value for consumers and retailers. *Journal of Retailing and Consumer Services, 21*(6), 1001–1012.

Vlad, M. 2011. Thinking human: Permission based mobile marketing can help lead the way. *International Journal of Mobile Marketing, 6*(2), 113–123.

Watson, C., McCarthy, J. & Rowley, J. 2013. Consumer attitudes towards mobile marketing in the smartphone era. *International Journal of Information Management, 33*(5), 840–849.

Wheeler, W.D. 2016. Slaves of vision: The virtual reality world of oculus rift. *Quarterly Review of Film and Video, 33*(6), 501–510.

Winn, W.D. 1995. *Semiotics and the design of objects, actions and interactions in virtual environments*. Washington, DC: Air Force Office of Scientific Research; U.S. West Foundation, 21.

Workman, J.E. & Caldwell, L.F. (2007). Centrality of visual product aesthetics, tactile and uniqueness needs of fashion consumers. *International Journal of Consumer Studies, 31*, 589–596.

Zhu, Y.Q. & Chen, H. 2015. Social media and human need satisfaction: Implications for social media marketing. *Business Horizons, 58*, 335–345.

6 Challenges in Luxury Marketing

Charity

Charity refers to humanitarian support to the less fortunate. Charities receive money from donors, partners, and businesses and in turn develop programs and strategies to benefit a demographic segment of their choice. Several factors can motivate businesses to engage in charitable expenditures such as firm size, industry, tax rates, managerial preferences for charity, ownership characteristics of the firm, and the availability of resources to businesses (Brammer, Millington, & Pavelin 2006). Usually, businesses combine charitable activities with promotion of brands for mass media attention. It can be argued: Why do luxury brands need to associate with a charity or philanthropic activities? Luxury brands do not need such attention, as they are often considered recession-proof and immune to market swings. Yet, luxury brands engage in corporate philanthropic and charitable activities in an inconspicuous manner, remain an icon, and thrive under a lack of exposure. Montblanc, Mercedes-Benz, Tiffany & Co, Cartier, and Four Seasons, among others, have significant connections to charitable activities and philanthropic projects that are cause-based and beneficial to society in particular, and humanity in general. Thus, luxury brands are selective in how they fund their charitable work, what benefits they expect from collaborating with a charity organization, and how the underlying image of the company and brand is supported by the outcome of the charitable work. In many cases, luxury brands are hesitant to link their image with a cause because of the inherent nature of the conflict (profit versus charity), and thus they need to attain a delicate balance between their desire to contribute to charitable activities and the need to get a higher long-term return on investment in a subtle manner.

Cultural Events and Institutions

Luxury brands undertake various philanthropic activities to promote different causes. For example, Louis Vuitton Moët Hennessey (LVMH), the parent company of Louis Vuitton and one of the largest luxury groups in the world with sales of about $3b and a head office in France, identifies itself within its creative communities by tying its identity to local culture. Its support for approximately 50 exhibitions in France—country of origin—and around the world has enabled millions of visitors to discover seminal periods in the history of art and enjoy the works of eminent and contemporary artists. LVMH aims to tie the country image and product quality to brand image, which necessitates the identification of how global consumers perceive the redefined concept of country of origin. The concept relates to a buyer's keen interest in status or self-image reinforcement provided by the luxury. Louis Vuitton may signify France, as it is often associated with the elegant French culture and luxury standard (Godey, Pederzoli, Aiello, Donvito, Chan, Oh, Singh, Skorobogatykh, Tsuchiya, & Weitz 2012). Louis Vuitton may be perceived as ethnocentric yet global.

Corporate Philanthropy

Luxury brands partner with charitable societies to serve its corporate social responsibility. When a company donates to a charity, it reflects positively on the company from its own standpoint and also from the consumers' viewpoint. Such campaigns are beneficial to improve the image of the sponsoring firm and sales (Ross, Patterson, & Stutts 1992). However, charities and luxury brands do form partnerships reluctantly. Charities gain access to the brand, and the brand supports the charity's mission, which is aligned with the goals, beliefs, or visions of the brand. Although charity organizations may have many donors, luxury brands need to find a charity that meshes with their brand image and corporate strategy. A mismatch may lower brand image and the opinion of luxury consumers. Although luxury brands may need to engage with a charity as ordinary brands do, luxury brands also need to represent exclusiveness. Luxury brands are exclusive because of their high price and status, so partnering with charities may help soften luxury brands' image by bringing them down to a level that ordinary consumers can relate to. For example, Montblanc is a luxury brand and offers luxury pens, among other products. A partnership with UNICEF allows Montblanc to be more noticeable to consumers who would not normally be exposed to the brand. The aim is to expose luxury brands in a limited way so as to strike a balance between a brand's desire to increase its brand awareness and the need to preserve its accessibility, exclusivity, and desirability. It may be challenging to balance this delicately.

Community Development

Luxury brands develop community by developing talents in their industry. Chanel, a leading brand in luxury fashion, encourages people to support its philanthropic mission (through the Chanel Foundation), which is to advance women's and girls' independence and empowerment by increasing their access to economic resources and entrepreneurship opportunities, education, and training, leadership, and decision-making, as well as health and social protection. This approach reaches a demographic segment of girls and women who are ages 17–34. Chanel's approach is an example of associating its brand with the issue of female empowerment for community development. Similarly, Lamborghini and Fendi apprenticeships and protégé programs support skills development. By attributing the charitable work to the needs of the industry, brands can develop a strategic competitive advantage. This community development strategy may appeal to a certain type of luxury customer who cares about values and authenticity and thus may like to engage with luxury brands that align their aesthetics with values such as charity (Chang 2020). Thus, brands use charitable venues strategically to blend skills, art, heritage, culture, and sophistication to produce not only luxury brands that collaborate with artists, but also artists who cooperate with brands' publicity and public relations (Zaniol 2016).

Luxury Shame

Luxury shame relates to the guilty feeling of buying luxury products. Guilt may occur when customers realize that what they bought is three times someone's monthly salary, or the sports car they bought costs the same as a modest house, or the expenditure is just wasteful (Tangney, Miller, Flicker, & Barlow 1996; Vinelli 2009). So, people tend to justify their luxury purchases. Luxury brands overcome the challenge by partnering with charities or philanthropic ventures through donating a portion of the price of a luxury product to a certain charity, making consumers feel less guilty about their purchases, knowing that a portion of what they spent goes to helping people in need. Customers who buy charity-linked luxury products get the dual satisfaction of supporting a cause and owning the product itself (Ahn 2015). People are more inclined to act altruistically when their good deeds can be viewed by others (Wiepking, Scaife, & McDonald 2012). It has been found that customers felt less guilty about buying Rolex when it was associated with the Save the Children charity. Consumers bought more Godiva chocolates when the brand was associated with a charity. Consumers benefited from the good feeling of helping a charity and the consumption of a luxury chocolate (Hagtvedt & Patrick 2016). In another example, Bulgari donated 20 percent of its profits to an organization that helped children in need (Kim, Kim, & Kim 2014). Although people should not feel shame for being successful, wealthy, or more fortunate than others, the charitable aspect may replace the guilt and shame with a positive feeling of being privileged. A recent study found that 94 percent of respondents thought that luxury brands should be involved in philanthropy and that 63 percent of respondents expected them to be involved in a charity (King 2016). Consumers may seek luxury brands that make positive statements about who they are, what they would like to be, and perhaps which charity they donate to and support (Silverstein & Fiske 2003).

However, consumers may also care about to whom or what luxury brands donate (Davies, Lee, & Ahonkhai 2011). If luxury brands donate a percentage of their sales to charities whose values are consistent with consumers' values, then this brand-charity strategy may earn consumers' trust and positive perception towards their brand, which may increase sales (Robinson, Irmak, & Jayachandran 2012). Unlike regular brands that publicize cause-related marketing, luxury brands tend to remain silent about their charity activities. Luxury brands rely on their own ability to create value and sell rather than giving consumers a reason to purchase their products. Most consumers may not even know that the luxury brands are associated with charities.

Controversies

Luxury brands are susceptible to controversies for their contributions to communities. If charity is defined as providing benefits to the public and communities, then the most suitable ventures for luxury brands are to support and protect monuments and cultural and heritage sites for their corporate philanthropic image. Recently, many French luxury brands pledged to donate millions of euros for the restoration of the fire-ravaged Notre Dame Cathedral in Paris in 2019. Yet, they were criticized for their actions. It may be possible that this kind of criticism comes from people who dislike the existence of wealth rather than disliking philanthropy (Arnett 2019). However, luxury brands may attract positive attention by making donations to unrelated areas. For example, the Rolls Royce Dine on the Line Gala was held in support of allergy research, a non-controversial field of charitable funding. Because luxury brands thrive in the sense of exclusivity and rarity, it forces their charitable impacts to be dampened, as they wish to remain quiet.

Counterfeit Luxury Products

The luxury counterfeit industry poses a significant challenge to luxury products. It is estimated to be four times larger than the luxury industry. The counterfeit industry has a growth of about 7 percent annually, with sales over $900b (Elings, Keith, & Wukoson 2013). The gap between the rich and the poor creates a market for counterfeit products. Poor people aspire to look, dress, and own luxury products just as the wealthy do but are left with no option other than to buy counterfeit luxury products. Counterfeit products are desired by consumers who cannot afford the genuine expensive luxury products. So, counterfeit products fill the gap. As the gap continues to exist, makers of counterfeit luxury products are expected to sell more to this segment. Because of advanced manufacturing technologies, counterfeit products strikingly resemble legitimate luxury brands (Qian 2014). Ironically, some of these products are reported to have unique features that are superior to those of iPhone or BlackBerry, including a greater variety of functions, slimmer appearance, and higher system stability (Ahmed 2016). With counterfeit luxury products taking the appearance of a luxury brand, the idea of purchasing such a product becomes very enticing and satisfying for consumers. The more popular the luxury products are, the more likely that customers will purchase them (Stravinskiene, Dovaliene, & Ambrazeviciute 2013). Counterfeit products merely serve those consumers who would otherwise not be able to afford genuine luxury items. However, if luxury brands were to reduce their prices, which is unlikely, consumers then may find it unnecessary to settle for counterfeit luxury products, since genuine luxury brands would be within their reach. So, the presence of counterfeit products makes the genuine items *true* and *authentic*, adding to their desirability and value, and thus creating a greater willingness among wealthier clients to pay for original goods (Romani, Gistri, & Pace 2012).

Who Buys Counterfeit Products?

A variety of customers buy counterfeit luxury products. Some consumers knowingly buy such products, whereas others think they got a deal. People buy counterfeit products knowingly because of price, uniqueness, availability, and the value the brand image represents to the individual and others (Ahmed 2016). A counterfeit purchase can occur on two dimensions: *structure of action* or *purpose of action* (Gistri, Romani, Pace, Gabrielli, & Grappi 2009). *Structure of action* refers to when consumers can carry out an interpersonal act or they can exert an action over an object—for example, display of status to signal that they are above their peers. On the other hand, *purpose of action* refers to the aim of the consumption, either autotelic (regarding oneself) or instrumental—for example, purchasing a counterfeit Hublot watch to keep track of time. Although it may seem intuitive that people with less wealth purchase counterfeit luxury products, young consumers actually are also found to purchase such goods because of their self-ambiguity, value consciousness, emphasis on the opinion of others, and lack of consideration for ethical issues (Stravinskiene, Dovaliene, & Ambrazeviciute 2013). However, in the context of China, age does not appear to affect the propensity to purchase counterfeit products (Wang & Song 2013). Theoretically, if consumers' interests in these products outweigh their moral values, then they are more likely to purchase counterfeit products (Kollmannova 2012). It is about status and not about quality that consumers expect. So, the motivation to buy counterfeit products is to signal a higher status to peers and society. Availability of counterfeit luxury brands means consumers who previously could not afford the genuine articles are now able to purchase an alternative (Phau, Sequeira, & Dix 2009).

The Emerging Market Perspective

Consumers in developing countries and emerging markets are more likely to purchase counterfeit products to indicate status, power, and wealth. China is one of the largest markets ($8b) for luxury products; the country is also known for its counterfeit luxury product industry. Contrary to popular belief that Chinese consumers refrain from being materialistic, studies indicate that ex-socialist and communist countries have much higher levels of materialism than those found in advanced economies (Sun, D'Alessandro, & Johnson 2014). The ability of consumers to purchase counterfeit luxury products helps them fit into a higher social class, giving them a sense of belonging and acceptance within their social group. For example, acceptance, approval, and image management are viewed positively in wealthier Chinese society. Chinese cultural beliefs of *face consciousness* and the nation's economic state both support the desire to buy counterfeit and original luxury goods (Wan, Luk, Yau, Tse, Sin, Kwong, & Chow 2009). It is expected that the next generation of the newly rich in China will buy genuine luxury products to appreciate and display their money and success (Schroeder, Borgerson, & Wu 2014). Views on acceptance and approval may differ from country to country, but the goal of feeling empowered and gaining a high level of social status remains the same. Counterfeit luxury marketers use the same luxury brand management technique, called *democratic luxury*, which is defined as a luxury item that extraordinary people would consider ordinary, and ordinary people would find extraordinary (Kapferer & Bastien 2008). The lower prices and trendy designs in counterfeit products are very popular in the emerging markets of Asia, Africa, and Latin America. Kollmannova (2012) predicts that Europe will consume counterfeit goods and lose its intellectual property profits, whereas China will profit from producing such counterfeit products for markets like Europe. And then the Chinese would consume the originals.

Counterfeit Luxury Products Life Cycle

Research indicates that the counterfeit luxury product life cycle (CLPLC) has four stages. In the first stage, counterfeiters wait for luxury brands to release new products into the market and then check whether the products are worth imitating so as to be commercially viable. That is, the break-even point should be feasible. If so, counterfeiters apply the *reverse engineering method* to redesign and mimic the original product as closely as possible. In the second stage, depending upon the nature of the products (technical watches versus handicraft bags), counterfeiters use the flexible manufacturing system (FMS) or computer numerical control (CNC) machines or artisans (in some cases, disgruntled employees who left genuine luxury brands) to make the redesigned counterfeit products with almost no noticeable difference. In the third stage of the counterfeit promotion, coincidently, genuine luxury marketing benefits counterfeit marketers, because luxury brands may have used a celebrity to endorse the product (or an elegant model to promote it), which indirectly conjures the image of being rich, beautiful, and successful. Customers indeed wish to portray the image but by owning counterfeit luxury goods. At the same time, counterfeit luxury products also generate publicity for the genuine luxury brands, because copying luxury products legitimates their designs in that they are desirable and worth copying (Hilton, Choi, & Chen 2004). In the final stage, the online environment benefits counterfeit marketing. Initially, skeptics felt that online marketing of luxury products diminished exclusivity, elegance, and status. However, the opposite may also be true, as online shoppers are tech savvy, time starved, and very knowledgeable about the luxury products they intend to purchase. Counterfeit luxury brands also use online marketing to their advantage to target their segments by offering a wide variety of counterfeit luxury products that may not be available in stores or streets. The accessibility of online stores also attracts new customers, demographics, and regions. This explains why nearly a third of the sales of counterfeit luxury products is conducted over the Internet (Wang & Song 2013). Because most customers ignore or do not pay attention to details such as coarse stitching, or slight off color, or logo distortion, they succeed in purchasing counterfeit products and demonstrating a higher social status to their peers and society. In general, these consumers are aware of the downsides of counterfeit products but are more than willing to purchase these goods, regardless of authenticity, as it may boost their status (Li, Robson, & Coates 2014). When customers buy counterfeit goods, they get immense value and pleasure from their purchases, depending upon their previous knowledge about the original product. Although the consumers might have lacked the shopping experience, they might still be thrilled to satisfy their dream by purchasing a counterfeit luxury product. These products are far from taboo or undesirable. In fact, everyone is entitled to enjoy a great work of art or wear a fashionable item of clothing, irrespective of income (Juggessur & Cohen 2009).

Counterfeit Prevention

Counterfeit luxury products hinder the economy through tax evasion and undermine the research and development activities of manufacturers of genuine luxury goods. As industries have globalized their distribution and production operations, counterfeiting has become easier to sustain (Hilton, Choi, & Chen 2004). The Chinese brand Crocodile, which is similar to the French brand Lacoste, generated a profit of about $30m in 2013 (Jiang & Shan 2016). The counterfeit industry is so large that for every dealer caught and sentenced, five new dealers with even larger networks appeared (Hieke 2010). In some cases, even legitimate producers sell counterfeit products in gray or black markets or the online environment. So, policing is difficult, and time consuming too. Some luxury brands cancel their contracts with producers, whereas other luxury brands collaborate with the police to raid such producers and retailers. Hermès and Louis Vuitton have sued the online retailer Alibaba for the sale of counterfeit products for damages as high as $100m (Ebel 2016). Genuine luxury brands need to protect their differentiation potential of a rare and limited brand; otherwise, it can be easily lost if too many people pose with fake luxury products. Alibaba offers large quantities of luxury counterfeit products for a small fraction of what the genuine articles cost. Genuine brands face a massive challenge with regard to preventing counterfeit luxury production.

Corporate Social Responsibility

Corporate social responsibility (CSR) has emerged recently as a key purchasing criterion for many groups of consumers—in particular among women—who consider that being green, ethical, and socially responsible is important for luxury brands (Bevolo, Gofman, & Moskowitz 2009). Many pro-environmental organizations have amplified their opinions against luxury brands that exploit resources (Bendell & Kleanthous 2007). Critics demand that these luxury brands become more socially responsible by incorporating more mindful business practices that protect the biodiversity of the planet (Mohr, Webb, & Harris 2001). Consumers are also increasingly taking into account the brands' CSR records in their decisions to purchase products. In response, Starbucks issued guidelines to evaluate the monetary and ecological effects of their coffee production. Microsoft focuses its CSR on human rights and environmental sustainability. So, there is a growing fear among luxury brands that if they do not incorporate more socially responsible practices into their business models, opponents may harm their equity through violent attacks on their environmental and social misbehavior records, hurting further the brands' reputation and businesses (Cervellon & Carey 2012). Burberry was attacked for its poor CSR records through the "Bloody Burberry" campaign. As such, CSR campaigns could negatively affect luxury brands because of a disfluency between the self-enhancement estimation of a luxury brand and the self-transcendent estimation of CSR (Torelli, Monga, & Kaikati 2011).

Sustainability

Sustainability relates to meeting the resource needs of current and future generations without compromising the health of the ecosystems that provides these resources (Morelli 2011). Luxury brands sell products that are rare and resource dependent, and thus sustainability of resources is a concern (Kale & Öztürk 2016). This concern has become a barrier for many luxury brands because of increased pressure from governments, non-governmental organizations, and consumers who demand more sustainable products (Cervellon 2013). The luxury industry in particular is under scrutiny for its poor consideration of sustainability and environmental concerns (Bendell & Kleanthous 2007). Sustainable consumption promotes a frugal lifestyle that enables society to have access to resources for future generations. This conflicts with the appeal of luxury products that symbolize wealth and prestige (Cervellon & Carey 2012). So, there is a shift in luxury brands' positioning that highlights status to brands that incorporate sustainable business practices in their manufacturing process. But, it may be challenging for all luxury brands to fully engage in sustainable practices. Instead of buying luxury products to display their wealth, some consumers have begun acting in a paradoxical manner—that is, *going green to be seen* (Griskevicius, Tybur, & Van den Bergh 2010). For example, Tesla, a relatively new luxury car brand, embodies a green alternative while being expensive. Replacement of the Tesla battery alone can cost many times more than normal battery replacement. As such, cobalt, a rare resource, is needed to make batteries. Production of more batteries means more depletion of natural resources. It is also worth mentioning the use of child labor in the Congo for the production of batteries (Petroff 2018). Being green while being responsible is challenging for luxury brands.

An integral part of the luxury industry is to increase its consumption of luxury goods, and thus profit, but the increased consumption contrasts with sustainability, as it exponentially depletes the stock of sustainable resources (Berry 1994). The challenge for luxury brands is that if they switch to more sustainable practices, they may be perceived as sacrificing their brands' authenticity, whereas others may interpret these changes towards sustainability as simply greenwashing their luxury products (Grayson & Martinec 2004). It is a *sustainability silence* as only a few luxury brands have taken a proactive stance in sustainable development (Kapferer & Michaut-Denizeaut 2014).

A relatively weak association exists between luxury products and sustainable development. Luxury is related to superficiality and personal pleasure, whereas sustainable development is more linked to selflessness and ethics (Widloecher 2010). Although some luxury brands have responded to the concerns of consumers such as Gucci, which supports UNICEF by producing a specific line of accessories every year and giving 25 percent of its profits to the association (Achabou & Dekhili 2013), the majority of luxury brands appear to pay little to no regard to corporate ethics. Also, they are yet to report on the environmental impact of their operations. Luxury brands have been criticized for the lack of leadership in this regard (Bendell & Kleanthous 2007). Luxury brands can pave the way for redefining the luxury dream from being a selfish, individual dream to one that considers environmental concerns. To remain a leader versus mass goods in the future, luxury brands need to be sustainable in social and ecological terms. Today's consumers are able to use information technology and get brands' ethical histories quickly.

Ethics

Ethical consumption is reflected when a consumer has a sense of responsibility towards society and expresses these feelings by means of their own purchase behavior (De Pelsmacker, Driesen, & Rayp 2005). It is found that knowledge of the supply chain of luxury products is important to ethical consumers (Cervellon & Wernerfelt 2012). The purchase of a product that concerns certain ethical issues can be considered ethical consumption (Doane 2001). These consumers are aware of the ethical credentials of luxury brands and are concerned about the social impact of the supply chain on bringing a product to the market (Varey 2002). So, there is a rise in consumer awareness regarding the ethical implications—pollution, human rights, animal welfare, and child labor, among others—of the products they purchase (Crane & Matten 2007). Burberry was a recent subject of controversy relating to pollution. In an effort to maintain the selectivity and image of the Burberry brand, they decided to burn and destroy sellable products. However, because of backlash from environmental groups, Burberry in 2018 announced that it was ending the practice of destroying finished luxury products and will expand the practice of recycling, repairing, and donating unsaleable products. Perhaps it would have been more meaningful to auction the products and donate the revenues to a charity that would support artisans.

Advertisements

China is one of the largest and fastest-growing markets among emerging economies for luxury products and services. As a result, large cities in China are flooded with billboards of advertisements for luxury products. The government believed that the advertisements were too ostentatious and a reminder of the gap between rich and poor. As a result, luxury brands needed to remove words such as "luxury," "royal," "supreme," and "high class" from their billboards, or face a 30k Yuan ($4,000) fine, as these aspirational advertisements created a *politically* unhealthy climate (Moore 2011). The message was that these advertisements should not encourage a *foreign* lifestyle. In another emerging market in Brazil, city planners in São Paulo have banned all outdoor advertising such as billboards, neon signs, etc., arguing that their absence makes the city look clean. In a similar vein, Gucci got into trouble when one of its advertisements featured an image of an unhealthy and thin-looking model. Although Gucci responded that the perception of the model's appearance was to some extent a *subjective issue*, the Advertising Standards Authority disagreed, saying that the ad irresponsibly showed a model with a body that was disproportionate and overly thin (ASA 2016). Although government regulations or public perception can change over time about advertising standards, they do explain some of the challenges luxury brands face related to advertising either in advanced nations or emerging markets.

Conclusion

The purpose of the chapter was to demonstrate how luxury brands face challenges in marketing or engaging in publicity as a result of the very nature of luxury products and services—that is, being exclusive, subdued, and silent. Four areas of challenges were discussed: charity activities (e.g. cultural events, corporate philanthropy, community development, luxury shame, and controversies); counterfeit luxury products (e.g. who buys counterfeit products, the emerging markets perspective, counterfeit luxury product life cycle, and counterfeit prevention); corporate social responsibility (e.g. sustainability and ethics); and government advertisement regulations.

Experiential Learning

1. Choose 30 luxury and 30 ordinary brands and compare:
   a. Publicity strategies
   b. Corporate social responsibility strategies
   c. Challenges in advertising in advanced nations and emerging markets

References

Achabou, M. & Dekhili, S. 2013. Luxury and sustainable development: Is there a match? *Journal of Business Research*, 66(10), 1896–1903.

Ahmed, T. 2016. Countering counterfeit branding: Implications for public-sector marketing. *Journal of Nonprofit & Public Sector Marketing*, 28(3), 273–286.

Ahn, S. 2015. The effect of luxury product pricing on consumers' perceptions about CSR Activities. *Academy of Marketing Studies Journal*, 19(3), 1–14.

Arnett, G. 2019. How charitable are fashion's biggest companies? www.voguebusiness. com/companies/luxury-fashion-companies-charitable-donations [Accessed on July 2, 2020].

ASA 2016. The advertising standards authority. www.theguardian.com/media/2016/apr/06/gucci-ad-banned-unhealthily-thin-model-asa [Accessed on July 2, 2020].

Bendell, J. & Kleanthous, A. 2007. Deeper luxury. *WWF*. www.wwf.org. uk/deeper luxury [Accessed on July 2, 2020].

Berry, C.J. 1994. *The idea of luxury: A conceptual and historical investigation*. Cambridge, UK: Cambridge University Press.

Bevolo, M. & Gofman, A. & Moskowitz, H. 2009. Sustainability, higher margin opportunities and economic crises: Lessons from the global study of premium products. ESOMAR World Research paper.

Brammer, S., Millington, A. & Pavelin, S. 2006. Is philanthropy strategic? An analysis of the management of charitable giving in large UK companies. *Business Ethics: A European Review*, 15(3), 234–245.

Cervellon, M.C. 2013. Conspicuous conservation: Using semiotics to understand sustainable luxury. *International Journal of Market Research*, 55(5), 695–717.

Cervellon, M.C. & Carey, L. 2012. Consumer perceptions of 'green': Why and how consumers use eco-fashion and green beauty products. *Critical Studies in Fashion and Beauty*, 2(1/2), 77–98.

Cervellon, M.C. & Wernerfelt, A. 2012. Knowledge sharing among green fashion communities online: Lessons for the sustainable supply chain. *Journal of Fashion Marketing and Management*, 16(2), 176–192.

Chang, T. 2020. The next wave of philanthropic luxury retail. *Luxe Digital*. https://luxe.digital/business/digital-luxury-trends/next-wave-philanthropic-luxury-retail [Accessed on July 2, 2020].

Crane, A. & Matten, D. 2007. *Business ethics*. Oxford: Oxford University Press.

Davies, I.A., Lee, Z. & Ahonkhai, I. 2011. Do consumers care about ethical-luxury? *Journal of Business Ethics*, 106(1), 37–51.

De Pelsmacker, P., Driesen, L. & Rayp, G. 2005. Do consumers care about ethics? *Journal of Consumer Affairs*, 39(2), 363–385.

Doane, D. 2001. *Taking flight: The rapid growth of ethical consumerism*. London: New Economics Foundation.

Ebel, K. 2016. Is mediation an effective medium to resolve contributory trademark liability disputes in counterfeit luxury goods? *Dispute Resolution Journal*, 71(1), 137–150.

Elings, R., Keith, L.D., & Wukoson, G.P. 2013. Anti-counterfeiting in the fashion and luxury sectors: Trends and strategies. *Industry Insight*, 33–37.

Gistri, G., Romani, S., Pace, S., Gabrielli, V. & Grappi, S. 2009. Consumption practices of counterfeit luxury goods in the Italian context. *Journal of Brand Management*, 16(5–6), 364–374.

Godey, B.R., Pederzoli, D., Aiello, G., Donvito, R. Chan, P., Oh, H., Singh, R., Skorobogatykh, I.I., Tsuchiya, J. & Weitz, B. 2012. Brand and country-of-origin effect on consumers' decision to purchase luxury products. *Journal of Business Research*, 65(10), 1461–1470.

Grayson, K. & Martinec, R. 2004. Consumer perceptions of iconicity and indexicality and their influence and on assessments of authentic market offerings. *Journal of Consumer Research*, 31(2), 296–312.

Griskevicius, V., Tybur, J.M. & Van den Bergh, B. 2010. Going green to be seen: Status, reputation and conspicuous conservation. *Journal of Personality and Social Psychology*, 98(3), 392–404.

Hagtvedt, H. & Patrick, V.M. 2016. Gilt and guilt: Should luxury and charity partner at the point of sale? *Journal of Retailing*, 92(1), 56–64.

Hieke, S. 2010. Effects of counterfeits on the image of luxury brands: An empirical study from the customer perspective. *Journal of Brand Management*, 18(2), 159–173.

Hilton, B., Choi, C.J. & Chen, S. 2004. The ethics of counterfeiting in the fashion industry: Quality, credence and profit issues. *Journal of Business Ethics*, 55(4), 343–352.

Jiang, L. & Shan, J. 2016. Counterfeits or Shanzhai? The role of face and brand consciousness in luxury copycat consumption. *Psychological Reports*, 119(1), 181–199.

Juggessur, J. & Cohen, G. 2009. Is fashion promoting counterfeit brands? *Journal of Brand Management*, 16(5/6), 383–394.

Kale, G.Ö. & Öztürk, G. 2016. The importance of sustainability in luxury brand management. *Intermedia International e-Journal*, 3(4), 106–126.

Kapferer, J. & Bastien, V. 2008. The specificity of luxury management: Turning marketing upside down. *Journal of Brand Management*, 16(5/6), 311–322.

Kapferer, J. & Michaut-Denizeaut, A. 2014. Is luxury compatible with sustainability? Luxury consumers' viewpoint. *Journal of Brand Management*, 21(1), 1–22.

Kim, M., Kim, D. & Kim, J. 2014. CSR for sustainable development: CSR beneficiary positioning and impression management motivation. *Corporate Social Responsibility and Environmental Management*, 21(1), 14–27.

King, J. 2016. 94pc of consumers say luxury should be involved with philanthropic causes: Bain. www.luxurydaily.com/94pc-of-consumers-say-luxury-should-be-involved-with-philanthropic-causes-bain [Accessed on July 2, 2020].

Kollmannova, K. 2012. Fake product? Why not! Attitudes toward the consumption of counterfeit goods in cee as shown on the example of Slovakia. *Central European Business Review*, 23–28.

Li, N., Robson, A. & Coates, N. 2014. Luxury brand commitment: A study of Chinese consumers. *Marketing Intelligence & Planning*, 32(7), 769–793.

Mohr, L.A. & Webb, D.J. & Harris, K.E. 2001. Do consumers expect companies to be socially responsible? The impact of corporate social responsibility on buying behavior. *Journal of Consumer Affairs*, 35(1), 45–72.

Moore, M. 2011. www.telegraph.co.uk/news/worldnews/asia/china/8398097/China-bans-luxury-advertising-in-Beijing.html [Accessed on July 2, 2020].

Morelli, J. 2011. Environmental sustainability: A definition for environmental professionals. *Journal of Environmental Sustainability*, 1(1), 1–9.

Petroff, A. 2018. Carmakers and big tech struggle to keep batteries free from child labor. https://money.cnn.com/2018/05/01/technology/cobalt-congo-child-labor-car-smartphone-batteries/index.html [Accessed on July 2, 2020].

Phau, I., Sequeira, M. & Dix, S. 2009. Consumers' willingness to knowingly purchase counterfeit products. *Direct Marketing: An International Journal*, 3(4), 262–281.

Qian, Y. 2014. Brand management and strategies against counterfeits. *Journal of Economics & Management Strategy*, 23(2), 317–343.

Robinson, S., Irmak, C. & Jayachandran, S. 2012. Choice of cause in cause-related marketing. *Journal of Marketing*, 76(4), 126–139.

Romani, S., Gistri, G. & Pace, S. 2012. When counterfeits raise the appeal of luxury brands. *Marketing Letters*, 23(3), 807–824.

Ross, P.J.K., Patterson, L.T. & Stutts, M.A. 1992. Consumer perceptions of organizations that use cause-related marketing. *Journal of the Academy of Marketing Science*, 20(1), 93–97.

Schroeder, J.E., Borgerson, J.L. & Wu, Z. 2014. A brand culture approach to brand literacy: Consumer co-creation and emerging Chinese luxury brands. *SSRN Electronic Journal*, 42, 366–370.

Silverstein, M. & Fiske, N. 2003. Luxury for the Masses. *Harvard Business Review*, 81(4), 48–57.

Stravinskiene, J., Dovaliene, A. & Ambrazeviciute, R. 2013. Factors influencing intent to buy counterfeits of luxury goods. *Economics and Management*, 18(4), 761–768.

Sun, G., D'Alessandro, S. & Johnson, L. 2014. Traditional culture, political ideologies, materialism and luxury consumption in China. *International Journal of Consumer Studies*, 38(6), 578–585.

Tangney, J., Miller, R., Flicker, L. & Barlow, D. 1996. Are shame, guilt, and embarrassment distinct emotions? *Journal of Personality and Social Psychology*, 70(6), 1256–1269.

Torelli, C.J., Monga, A.B. & Kaikati, A.M. 2011. Doing poorly by doing good: Corporate social responsibility and brand concepts. *Journal of Consumer Research*, 38(5), 948–963.

Varey, R. 2002. *Marketing communication: Principles and practice*. London: Routledge.

Vinelli, R. 2009. Luxury shame: An emerging norm. *SSRN Electronic Journal*, February, 1–20.

Wan, W.W.N., Luk, C.L., Yau, O.H.M., Tse, A.C.B., Sin, L.Y.N., Kwong, K.K. & Chow, R.P.M. 2009. Do traditional Chinese cultural values nourish a market for pirated CDs? *Journal of Business Ethics*, 88, 185–196.

Wang, Y. & Song, Y. 2013. Counterfeiting: Friend or foe of luxury brands? An examination of Chinese consumers' attitudes toward counterfeit luxury brands. *Journal of Global Marketing*, 26(4), 173–187.

Widloecher, P. 2010. Luxe Et Développement Durable: Je T'aime, Moi Non-Plus? *Luxefrancais*.

Wiepking, P., Scaife, W. & McDonald, K. 2012. Motives and barriers to bequest giving. *Journal of Consumer Behaviour*, 11(1), 56–66.

Zaniol, G. 2016. Brand art sensation: From high art to luxury branding. *Cultural Politics*, 12(1), 49–53.

Part II
Fashion Marketing

7 Fashion Marketing

Political Fashion

Clothing serves purposes beyond protecting our bodies. It may indicate tribe, ethnicity, religion, identity, self-expression, status, wealth, or political views (Yangzom 2016). A person's choice of clothing influences the impression they create and transmit. Therefore, it serves as a powerful communication tool (Howlett, Pine, Orakçioglu, & Fletcher 2013). Clothing and, by extension, fashion (i.e. what we wear, or type of clothes we wear) is a means of non-verbal communication in our everyday lives. Fashion may be seen as superficial and ephemeral, while others may find it logical and natural to convey the wearer's status, wealth, religion, cultural background, or political views (Meinhold & Irons 2013). Fashion is an excellent method of communication, because it is quick and easy to make adjustments as the conversation changes. But messages should be clear. In 2018, US First Lady Melania Trump wore a jacket on a visit to immigrant children. Words on the back of the jacket read: *I really don't care, do you?* The purpose of this message was allegedly in response to media critics telling them she did not care about their message; however, the message was interpreted as she did not care about immigrant children, a very divisive topic at that time (Mark 2018). Recently, US Congressional Democrats were criticized for wearing *kente*—a traditional African textile whose origins are believed to stretch back to later than 1000 BC—during a moment of silence for George Floyd (an African American allegedly killed by a white US police officer), and using it as a political prop (Lee 2020). Individuals and groups use clothing as a means to broadcast their opinions, whether it is a message on a T-shirt or an entire ensemble. Indeed, people often proclaim their allegiances—political, cultural, religious, and professional—by the way they dress (Miller 2005). The first impression may also be the lasting impression.

Social Issues

Every item of dress, no matter how humble, dignified, frivolous, or vanguard, occupies space in fashion (Leitch 1996). Self-decoration is a part of self-constitution, body image, and identity formation. Fashion has come under scrutiny in Western society for the over-sexualization of people (Edwards 2018). This has led women to fight for their rights to wear clothing of their choice, reinforcing their belief that clothing should not be viewed as reflecting a sexualized outlook. Such labeling of women may be shameful. The sexualization of people, particularly women, has become political in nature. Fashion has been used to connect and recognize others in terms of whether they stand with one or against one in political opinions. Whether it was Hillary Clinton wearing a white pantsuit referencing the suffragette movement during her presidential debates or Beyoncé's backup dancers embodying the Blank Panther image at the Super Bowl, fashion has been a way to assert an identity and brand groups with similar ideologies (Friedman 2016). Clothing fashion is used as a channel for raising awareness of social and political issues and to convey to people certain thoughts and ideas. Political fashion is just another way for people to highlight current issues in society. Protesters of all stripes—feminists, white supremacists, Antifa, nationalists, and social justice advocates—outfit themselves to match their political mindsets (Delgado 2018). Fashion can be used as an outlet to express opinions on social issues that the wearers believe in strongly enough to publicly display on their bodies. Clothing can be used to denote political statements, such as rainbow paraphernalia to support LGBTQ movements, etc., or to subvert the political agenda being enforced, such as in China and Russia where vocal expression is denounced.

Governments

Governments and politics have direct influence on fashion. A government can restrict the supply of materials or outside resources that deviate fashion from traditional cultural practices (Obukhova, Zuckerman, & Zhang 2014). Government rules and regulations have a direct impact on citizens' everyday life and dress code (Thucydides 2017). North Korea's restriction on hairstyle and clothing choices, Saudi Arabia's full coverage laws for women, and the freedom of dress in many Western countries are some examples. In fact, there are government-approved hairstyles for residents of North Korea that reflect the government's political agenda (Smith 2018). So, governments may use fashion as a cultural and social medium to transform the consumer behavior of their citizens. If people begin to think about one aspect of their lifestyle, they may also become aware of other aspects of their lifestyle. For example, if women see restrictive clothing requirements as an infringement of their rights, they may also see how much further that restrictive control over their rights may bleed into other aspects of their lives. This domino effect may lead to protests or lobbying to reduce those laws and regulations (Hirscher & Niinimaki 2013). In another example of making a political statement through fashion, designers used the London Fashion Week as a platform to express their dissatisfaction with the news of Brexit. In their fashion collection, the designers fused both Western and Indian styles and featured models with painted faces done in traditional Indian-style makeup to convey the message of diversity and inclusion (Tan 2017).

Freedom Protest

In an effort to revitalize handicraft traditions and further themselves from Britain, India used the political significance of the *khadi* as a way to achieve freedom. This hand-spun type of cloth was used by Mahatma Gandhi as a way of both retaliating against British imported cloth and promoting Indian self-reliance (Khaire 2011). The shift away from British exports towards local craftsmanship in the clothing industry had a positive impact on the country's social and economic welfare. Khadi is still worn by political leaders in India. Activists also wear it. In fact, wearing fashionable khadi is trendy and expensive. In Tibet, where expressing any view can be considered being in opposition to the government, the distinct clothing serves as a subtle way to send a message without the repercussions of actually speaking up and defying authority (Yangzom 2016). Social media, where images with distinct fashion are a simple way to get information across to millions of people with relative ease, is a new tool with tremendous communications potential. In fact, the Euromaidan demonstrations in Ukraine used Instagram to document the riots in real time. Journalists also used it to determine where the action was happening (Sadof 2017).

Political Branding

Brands begin and end with people (Eckersley 2004). Branding is essentially a science that requires careful linking of a brand message to the end consumer. Like products, political leaders also brand themselves about what they stand for in the community. The voters are their customers. Like any other brand, politicians need to brand their message for their voters. Political leaders are strategic brands in a political landscape (Bigi, Treen, & Bal 2016). Their customer orientation is based on whether they ignore their voters, serve their voters, shape their voters, or have dialogue with voters. A type of political leader reflects a type of branding. They themselves are the political statements to which their voters react. Celebrities (as a brand endorser) often make political statements or support political movements in a public manner, and oftentimes encourage their fans and supporters to support the same. Politicians use fashion statements (such as Donald Trump's *Make America Great Again* [MAGA] fashion cap) to affect their fan base. Natalie Portman recently sported a *Make America Gay Again* hat (in the same fashion as Trump's cap) at a women's rally. In another instance, the color of the hat was changed to black to target the African American community and their social issues. Clothing has been a means of solidifying a group identity when faced with disparate views (Yangzom 2016). Most famous politicians have used fashion, whether a distinct fashion or ethnic clothing (e.g. Libya's former president, Colonel Muammar Gaddafi, India's Mahatma Gandhi, and Afghanistan's President Hamid Karzai, among others) or hairstyle (e.g. India's Prime Minister Indira Gandhi, Ukraine's presidential candidate Yulia Tymoshenko, among others) to stand out among other politicians as a recognizable brand. Recently, US Congresswoman Rashida Tlaib chose to wear a *thobe* (traditional Palestinian dress) during her congressional swearing-in ceremony. It is like a political logo, brand, and statement. Although branded politicians and celebrities can affect people's political viewpoint, in the 2004 US presidential election, many famous individuals and musicians failed to influence their fans through various media outlets not to vote to re-elect George W. Bush (Jackson 2008).

Cultural Appropriation

In North America, Indigenous designers are utilizing the fashion runways and protesting to highlight the issue of cultural appropriation and misconceptions about their culture. It may be important for fashion houses to get involved in a way that supports the culture on a long-term basis (Allaire 2018). The fashion industry has a record of co-opting political and countercultural movements, marginalized groups, and non-Western cultures, and they do make a profit out of it. It is not wrong for the fashion industry to cash in on the newest buzz word, but more often than not, this can lead to cultural irrelevance (Delgado 2018). Fashion is a kind of meeting point for many aspects of culture.

Effectiveness

Fashion has been instrumental in defining the self (Buckley & Clark 2012). What one wears is used as a tool for self-expression, individuality, and personal style. It can further be used to connect individuals or groups with similar tastes (Hirscher & Niinimaki 2013). Fashion draws on deeply rooted human values, ideals, and desires, such as values and symbols of social recognition and fashion, and is one of the most powerful and direct expressions of personal aspiration, individuality, and belonging (Howlett, Pine, Orakçioglu, & Fletcher 2013). Naturally, people admire and draw inspiration from others by the way they dress. This process becomes politicized, although less universal, when clothes are used to express solidarity with others. In some cases, it is reasonable to suggest that clothes may not create strong, effective bonds for political actions because clothes can be worn to impress, deceive, or confuse. They might be worn misleadingly or be misread by observers also (Miller 2005). This may be illustrated at the 2014 Winter Olympics in Sochi when the German team wore rainbow-colored uniforms, with many believing that this was done intentionally in retaliation against Russia's anti-gay propaganda law; however, the German Olympic Sports Confederation dismissed this, stating that the uniforms held no political weight or pro-gay message. Indeed, fashion also changes quickly, and people tend to go back to their own style.

Eco Fashion

The term *eco fashion* refers to clothing that has been manufactured using sustainable methods or resources to minimize negative environmental externalities that are otherwise associated with clothing production (Chan & Wong 2012). Eco fashion differentiates from other fashion products. With environmental concern growing worldwide, eco fashion is a desirable alternative to traditional production systems. Eco-fashion firms include environmental sustainability in their business processes, satisfy both internal and external stakeholders, and contribute to a superior business performance. For example, an eco-fashion firm can invest in green manufacturing methods but save on waste disposal fees while mitigating the waste's negative impact on the environment (Esty & Winston 2006). Raw material sourcing, manufacturing methods, and waste disposal can be considered while still producing the highest-quality products. Environmental degradation weighs heavily on the hearts and minds of people across the world. Therefore, the emotional connection is important in marketing eco-fashion products as a lifestyle.

Firms can create value by going green. Value creation in eco fashion is much more prevalent in advanced countries than in emerging markets. Consumers in advanced countries appear to place a higher value on quality of life and are more conscious of environmental hazards than consumers in emerging markets, who resist paying a premium for eco-fashion products. Luxury fashion brands can take steps to implement the concept of eco fashion into their production without sacrificing quality. Stella McCartney manufactures desirable eco-fashion pieces. Its overarching mission reflects respect for the environment. The brand uses organic cotton across its product collections, has eliminated the use of pesticides, and conserves a huge amount of water (SMC 2018). Apparel made from bamboo in Cambodia is gaining traction for its cooling effects during summer. By paying attention to social and environmental sustainability, financial returns can be rewarding (Wilson 2015).

Competitive Advantage

The term *eco luxury* refers to the creation of an emotional connection between the consumer and luxury brand using a sincere approach (Gibson & Seibold 2014). Eco fashion can be the approach. The luxury fashion market is saturated with global brands selling high-cost, high-quality products to loyal customer bases. The brand loyalty and exclusivity accompanying the luxury fashion market makes it difficult to penetrate. To become a key player in this specific market, one needs to find a niche to differentiate their products and brands. Because of changing global perception and values regarding concern for the environment, eco fashion can differentiate itself from the competition and, in fact, can create competitive advantage. Luxury fashion items are purchased and adorned as a way to portray success. An eco-competitive advantage can be created without sacrificing product quality or the exclusiveness of its image. Consumers can still portray an image of high status and success. Luxury fashion brands have the means and resources to implement a green manufacturing business model such as sourcing more sustainable textiles. Luxury consumers want the brands that they adorn themselves with to reflect their ambition for a more sustainable world both socially and environmentally (Bendell & Kleanthous 2007). However, a contradiction may exist between people viewing luxury as unnecessary and therefore *wasteful*, and viewing sustainability as eco-friendly and therefore *sustainable luxury* (Cervellon & Shammas 2013). It is true that quality eco-fashion products are also expensive because of the higher costs associated with environmentally sustainable textiles and manufacturing of clothing. Thus, many consumers cannot support this initiative (Ruoh-Nan, Karen, & LaVon 2012). So, the alternative could be fast fashion.

Fast Fashion

The purpose of fast fashion is to provide consumers who cannot afford luxury fashion with a less expensive alternative to make them feel included in current fashion trends. These products are cheaper, trendy, and attractive, designed to satisfy customers' desires rather than necessity. Generally, fast fashion items are purchased with less regard for other factors such as environmental impact or function versus style; they are bought solely to fulfill the desire to be considered fashionable (Kim, Ho, & Yoon 2013). Fast fashion production turnover is rapid to coincide with the changing seasons and trends sought by customers. They are also rapidly obsolete because of fluctuations in fashion trends, usually from socio-cultural changes in consumers of high-fashion items (Gabrielli, Baghi, & Codeluppi 2013). Because of the short product life cycle of fast fashion, customers are under pressure to make timely purchasing decisions. They may also think that buying more for less is a much better option than paying higher prices for high-quality items but having fewer of them. The availability of fast fashion is a deterrent to consumers purchasing more expensive, high-quality eco-fashion clothing (Niinimäki 2010). Customers are also more likely to dispose of cheap, mass-produced clothes (e.g. fast or fad fashion) than more expensive items (e.g. eco or luxury fashion). Fast fashion production is a standardized process that minimizes the manufacturing and transportation time needed to reach consumers. Internal processes, such as sourcing, buying, merchandising, and making swift decisions regarding fashion collections, are also streamlined (Bruce & Daly 2006). So, implementing environmentally sustainable methods to produce eco-fashion products disrupts the current system and its efficiency, resulting in higher production costs. As manufacturers and suppliers are meshed within the system, any changes to the production process needs to be coordinated with external agents, further reducing efficiency. Thus, eco fashion may create competitive advantages in marketing luxury products but *not* in the fast fashion sector. In fast fashion, trends and attractiveness of items create value and sales. However, the challenge is to get fast fashion and its value known quickly, that is, within the next season. In short, the global fashion industry generates a huge amount of waste. In fact, one full garbage truck of clothes is burned or sent to a landfill every second (EMF 2017). The clothier H&M announced a plan to make all its apparel from recycled or sustainably sourced materials by 2030. It is also testing its *repair and remake* stations in select stores and *clothing rentals* in Stockholm (Gerretsen & Kottasova 2020).

Colors in Fashion

Fashion clothing uses colors to grab attention or convey meaning (Kauppinen-Raisanen & Luomala 2010). Colors have been used in many social movements globally (Sawer 2007). From gay liberation to women's rights, colors have been a fundamental part of fashion, particularly to represent social movements. Black Pride, the Orange Revolution in Ukraine, the Marcus Garvey movement and its Rastafarian colors, and the LGBTQ movement with its rainbow colors (although it used a pink triangular symbol in the past) are some examples of the colors being used as communication tools. Color has been instrumental in the fashion of social movements, with groups of people often coordinating efforts to stand in solidarity. Although political movements can be branded using colors, political movements are centered on social issues, and the representative colors may not necessarily reflect any particular meaning directed at the movement, but more so at the brand itself. Further, colors are entirely subjective, so one person's association may not be that of another's (Nitse, Parker, Krumwiede, & Ottaway 2004). Use of colors is a pervasive and widely used marketing and advertising tool. Certain colors, patterns, or otherwise notable distinguishing features are often attributed to a particular social issue. Colors' meanings are context dependent as well (Won & Westland 2016).

Ethnic Fashion

Ethnic wear is different from Western fashion. Western fashion changes frequently and projects individual identity, whereas ethnic fashion is permanent and traditional, encodes deep meanings, and projects group identity, relationship, and membership (Rovine 2009). Ethnic wear plays a fundamental role in forming status, preserving culture, and displaying national identity. Ethnic wear is a symbol of preserving identity and a proof of an ethnocentric culture in the face of globalization and adversity (Strübel 2012). In the context of globalization, the Edun brand (now in the LVMH group) was founded by Hewson and Bono to source and promote trade in Africa. According to social identity theory, ethnic wear serves as a means of identifying an ethnic group or a cluster of people that share commonalities. Ethnic wear is also an expression of pride in one's origin and heritage. As cultures begin to assimilate in different parts of the world, ethnic groups, who have emigrated from their homelands, tend to hold on to their origins, although they lose a much of their ancestral identity by moving to another country (Naujoks 2010). Thus, to protect the further loss of ancestral identity, ethnic groups use symbolic identity or visual representations in the form of ethnic wear. So, ethnic wear serves as a connection between ethnic culture and the origin of their identity. Because of the inevitable rise of globalization, consumers tend to become more homogenous in their choices, and therefore marketers may prefer a global marketing strategy to selling ethnic wear. It can also be argued that, because of homogenization, people are now more concerned with their global identity than their ethnic background, and thus even ethnic groups may want to be a part of the global village.

In Japan, about 80 percent of women depicted in clothing advertisements are Caucasian compared with 7 percent Asian. Although it can be argued that ethnic Japanese models can yield a more ethno-driven demand, the depiction of Caucasian models may be interpreted by Japanese women as a sign of a global identity. Caucasian models in advertisements improved self-image, whereas Asian models presented everyday products (Morimoto & Chang 2009). From a global perspective, Caucasian women in advertisements seem to be associated with power, freedom, and wealth, which many ethnic identities aspire to have. Caucasian female models wearing ethnic clothing were found to be in high-end fashion magazines even though the majority of Japanese women wore ethnic dresses on a regular basis. Ethnic fashion may be a source of inspiration for many global designer brands, yet they creatively market their apparel as a symbol of identity retention, nationalism, and tradition (Yu, Kim, Lee, & Hong 2001).

Gender Differences

Gender identity theory refers to the personality traits of masculinity and femininity (Heather & Weber 2012). The theory explains the significance of gender differences in global and local marketing strategy of ethnic wear. A study in Chinese, Japanese, and Korean context finds that female consumers score higher on aesthetic, religious, and ethnic clothing values than male consumers, but female consumers score lower on economic and political and clothing values than male consumers. Additionally, these three ethnic groups display distinct reference group influence, media difference, and store attribute importance; however, these patterns differ depending on the level of acculturation (Hsu & Burns 2012). Men and women have different tastes in terms of consumption style such as clothing choice and media preference, among others (Lee, Fairhurst, & Dillard 2002). So, the choices are made based on their level of acculturation, strength of ethnic identification, and family background. Women seem to like ethnic fashion more than men. In Kuwait, it appears that men like to wear Western-fashion clothes like jeans and T-shirts more than women (Kelly 2010). It may be that women may have more ethnic fashion choices available than men, or unlike women, men are not given instructions for wearing ethnic clothing such as *Palestinian scarf* or *checkered scarf* or *African scarf*, for example. African women wear *headscarves* for religious and cultural reasons and even as a fashion statement, but they are traditionally worn by older, usually married, women (Fihlani 2016). Qatari and Saudi ethnic groups like to gather ethnic wear information through traditional reference sources and family members and friends, the most frequently used information sources being traditional store displays, non-traditional videos, and TV (Cardona & Rabolt 1997). Women may have more ethnic fashion clothing education and information available than men (Akou 2007).

Education

Education is important to value ethnic wear. For example, the *kimono* in Japan is an alternative to Western clothing. It is interesting that some kimono schools emphasize ethnic values such as harmony and group orientation, making girls feel proud of their ethnicity, and local family tradition, after purchasing either a new or a used kimono (Assmann 2008). By learning how to properly wear ethnic clothes and how to appropriately behave in ethnic wear as part of the community network, local people are more attracted to the ethnic wear that matches their ethnic aesthetic sensibility. However, education may not always influence choice of ethnic wear as educated people may not use traditional media to get information about traditional ethnic wear (Cardona & Rabolt 1997). So, for the educated segment of the ethnic wear market, modern global media should be an effective marketing strategy, whereas for the other segment, local TV or sales calls should be equally effective. A localized marketing strategy for ethnic wear strengthens the sense of identity and cultural belonging, whereas a global marketing strategy supports global fashion without compromising one's connection to their ethnic origins. The glocalized strategy reinforces the sense of ethnic community while maintaining its continuity and competitiveness in the global fashion market.

Beachwear

The global beachwear market is diverse and one of the fastest-growing markets, expected to be worth $28b in 2027 (GIA 2020). Growth in the sector is fueled by increased trade liberalization and people's ability to travel freely to coastal destinations. As a result, beachwear is being marketed as casual wear such as shorts that can be purchased year-round. Growth of the beauty and spa industry has also fueled the growth of beachwear, as the demand for specialty beachwear has led to the rise of novelty swimwear producers (Angelis 2013). Further, the aging population and baby boomers of North America have created a large market of consumers with a high level of purchasing power who desire high-quality products, which are historically tied to hefty profits in the beachwear industry (Davis 2009). The profit is high because of the premium value to required cloth ratio. The growing rate of obesity across North American and European countries has also led to an increase in the demand for plus-size beachwear, a market that has largely been ignored. Brazil is one of the largest beachwear and bikini markets in the world because of the yearlong beachwear season combined with a host of large local producers that offer a wide selection of innovative products at a variety of price points. China is also one of the fastest-growing markets for beachwear, with an annual increase of about 8 percent (GIA 2020). Clearly, the future for the beachwear market is promising.

Seasonality

Length of season affects beachwear sales. So, beachwear can be regarded as seasonal apparel. Countries with year-round sunlight are more likely to have greater selling opportunities of beachwear than countries with short seasons. Thus, consumers in countries that have noticeable changes in seasonal climates are more inclined to purchase weather-appropriate apparel. Consumers who are influenced by fashion trends are likely to pay more for beachwear as they may need to replace it or get new beachwear, because either the style is outdated or the item no longer fits properly (Easey 2009). Seasonality also creates challenges for marketing managers in that they need to introduce products as soon as possible after market information has been collected. However, managers can forecast beachwear market trends on the basis of successful beachwear introduction in other countries with similar warmer climates and then try to introduce those trends in seasonal countries at the appropriate time in hopes of replicating the same level of success. Firms such as Marks & Spencer test their summer ranges in the Middle East. Countries that hold similar social and cultural values may have similar responses to fashion trends and market fluctuations. Therefore, it can be implied that a particular product can have an identical level of success, or failure, across these markets (Lea-Greenwood 2013). On the other hand, in countries that have dissimilar cultural values, managers need to adjust the marketing mix and communication channels. Similarly, in countries that have a consistent climate, consumers can still be open to fashion changes or trends (Sproles 1981). Managers can also pick up fashion beachwear trends from previous years and determine whether demand for these products still exists or whether they warrant adaptation.

Culture

The term *culture* is the collective preprogramming of the mind that distinguishes one group from another (Hofstede 2001). In the context of beachwear marketing, we focus on collective and individualistic cultures as the differences between the two have a significant impact on how consumers select fashion designs and trends. Collectivistic cultures relate to the status of the social system in which people see themselves as a part of the system. In this culture, the distinction between self and the social milieus is blurred, and thus greater communication between members of these social systems flows (Bochner 1994). In collectivistic cultures, efficiency in communications allows marketing managers to focus on the most popular design trends to effectively reach a large portion of the social system (Hall 1976). This system leads to consumers selecting a few unique styles as they wish to make choices in line with the pre-established designs and trends in their social and culture systems. In contrast, individualistic cultures have far fewer norms and regulations, thus leading to greater freedom to make decisions that may differ or run counter to the traditional views or actions of their culture. The desire to be unique and trendy leads consumers to purchase beachwear that may not be consistent with social norms, because consumers are more interested in setting themselves apart than blending in. People in this culture are much more open to new and foreign designs and trends, allowing marketers to use the different designs and trends to set them apart from the norms of the existing culture and making them appear unique or different (Doran 2002). Each continent should have its own beachwear marketing strategy based on culture, religion, and political factors.

Color

Color influences beachwear sales significantly as it satisfies customers' needs (Chang 1990; Deng, Hui, & Hutchinson 2010). For example, warm colors can elevate mood and spur activity, vitality, and arousal (Aaronson 1970). White is linked to sincerity and is often associated with purity, cleanliness, and peace (Mahnke 1996). Yellow is often viewed as a cheerful, optimistic, and friendly color (Fraser & Banks 2004), whereas pink is considered nurturing, warm, and soft (Clarke & Costall 2008). Blue indicates competence, trust, and logic (Wright 1988). Indeed, color preference is affected by regional cultural traits, and each country has its own sets of emotions and personalities associated with individual colors (Eunyoung 2007). Also, color preferences in fashion products are affected by national and regional traits (Choi, Shim, & Syn 2006). Thus, it can be expected that colorful (i.e. warm colors) beachwear is more likely to appeal to individuals in Africa than in Europe, where consumers prefer subdued and neutral colors (i.e. less-saturated colors). As such, consumer preferences change. Regardless of culture, some regions may emphasize the color of the beachwear, while others may value fabric, cut, and design (Posner 2011).

Nudity and Modesty

Nudity or a partially covered body may bring shame if it is not consistent with social and cultural norms. Clothing is a key component of patterns of sexually coded rules of conduct (Bansal 2008). Countries that do not overly emphasize modesty may tend to follow Western ideals of beachwear, which tends to be smaller and more revealing. However, in modest and conservative countries such as Turkey and Kuwait, beachwear is still sexually appealing but modestly covered—that is, loose fitting, open in the back, showing little to no cleavage, and provided with a long dress to cover most of the legs, along with a large shirt to cover the revealing clothing underneath. So, nudity is an important factor in deciding how marketing managers will advertise beachwear to consumers in conservative countries that may rely mainly on brand appeal and product features, whereas consumers in liberal countries may be more open to nudity or design-based appeals. Marketing managers need to strike a balance between the perceived value of the beachwear and frequency of its use (i.e. length of seasonality). Recently, beachwear has also been promoted as a fashion that can be worn by somebody who does not intend to swim but rather just wishes to walk on the beach in style. Luxury brands such as Louis Vuitton are suitable to target this new segment of beachgoers.

Undergarments

Modest beachwear used to be a necessity for the higher class to cover themselves when bathing or publicly swimming while differentiating themselves from the rest of society. In fact, women used to wear a bathing dress—almost covered head to toe—which was uncomfortable and hard to swim in (Poli 1995). Decades of slowly transitioning from full gowns to more form-fitting and sexier designs—developed in the 1940s during World War II—gave birth to the bikini, a radical design yet comfortable and beautiful. Since then, beachwear has become smaller and smaller and more and more revealing, almost resembling undergarments. Indeed, there was a time when undergarments were *unmentionables* and used for utility rather than for fashion (Bansal 2008). It took substantial changes in society for women in many countries to be able to wear beachwear expressively, confidently, and inclusively. Modern beachwear appears to resemble underwear and bikinis.

Age

Age plays a significant role in the underwear industry. Mintel (2004) shows that women who are driving sales—particularly of colorful and fashionable underwear and who have an underwear repertoire rather than just everyday underwear—are predominantly upper and middle class and under the age of 45. However, actual age is chronological, whereas cognitive age relates to one's self (Stephens 1991). A person's cognitive age may be more accessible and salient than a person's chronological age and thus more likely to be taken into account when making judgments. Therefore, it is challenging to decide whether to market underwear on the basis of chronological age or cognitive age. To make stylistic changes and to generate universal appeal, some local designers combined newly made pineapple cloths with silk and dyed them with various colors to develop a new cloth material and fabric, which were adaptive to contemporary fashion clothing (Chibnik,

Colloredo-Mansfeld, Lee, Milgram, Rovine, & Weil 2004). Because many fashion trends do not follow a logical progression based solely on quality, functionality, or price, the brand of the clothes or fabric may be a determining factor as to what is fashionable or not. Ethnic creativity favors unique and traditional colors and styles. Regardless, different age groups need different colors, designs, and sizes of clothing.

Changing Preferences

Well-fitted outfits render confidence and power to express individualistic style. Body shapes and changing social attitudes towards nudity, individuality, and human rights have forced the underwear spectrum of style and design to new levels. It is important to understand how the shape of diverse ethnic female consumers varies (Shin & Cynthia 2007). So, a global fit versus a custom fit is a significant issue for fashion brands, which benefit from economies of scale and standardization rather than fit (Vrontis & Vronti 2004). It is interesting to note how sales of Victoria's Secret products declined when the company struggled to adapt from its traditional reliance on push-up bras to women's expectation for well-fitted bras that were more comfortable. Women have been wearing underwire bras since the 1930s, but it seems they are falling out of love with lingerie with built-in scaffolding. There is a rise in appetite for soft silhouettes and functional comfort bralettes (Joyce 2018). As a result, women now shop more at ThirdLove, Lively, and American Eagle, which pitch inclusiveness and comfort over sex appeal by making custom-fitted bras (La Monica 2019). From offering a wider range of cup sizes and nude shades, to celebrating diversity in campaigns and on runways, intimate apparel labels are selling more than bras; they are selling inclusivity also (Rapp 2019). In fact, post-feminism argues for a discourse of liberation and sexual appeal (Amy-Chinn 2006). Women are embracing lingerie that encompasses alternative forms of sex appeal and increasingly buying from brands that prioritize body positivity, comfort, and proper fit. Although bralettes and sports bras are increasingly preferred to cleavage-enhancing push-up bras, Victoria's Secret still has the leading market share in the US.

Globally, the lingerie market is expected to earn more than $325b by 2025 (Marci 2020). One of the reasons for the rise in underwear sales, particularly luxury lingerie, is the Chinese market where people in influential positions realize that buying expensive luxury products might result in a belief that they and their families are involved in corruption. Communist cadres like to spend money, but on private pleasures such as gambling, luxury items, etc. (Hatton 2016). Luxury lingerie could be one of these items. For example, the Mouawad-designed Victoria's Secret Fantasy Bra and detachable belt—valued at $2m—feature more than 6,500 precious gems, including diamonds, yellow sapphires, and blue topaz set in 18-karat gold (Gustafson 2015). The fantasy bra may be suitable for the Chinese elite or someone with similar tastes.

The Internet contributes to sales because men do not have to go to women's shops to buy lingerie for gift-giving. Another vast lingerie market is the Middle East, where because of the religious distinction between inner and outer clothing, lingerie is often bright and garnished, as opposed to the anonymous drabness of the mainly black, gray, and blue *burkas* worn in public. In the West, outerwear is flamboyant, but in the Middle East or Islamic countries, flamboyancy is reserved for home (Halasa & Salam 2008). Some countries such as Syria did not even manufacture bras locally until 1970. Women used elastic bands instead. In contrast, the hillside town of Nova Friburgo is considered to be the lingerie capital of Brazil; it is home to more than 1,300 registered underwear retailers and manufacturers. Brazilian sensuality makes the lingerie market very appealing to foreigners. The town also attracts lingerie fashion enthusiasts (Guardian 2015). Albania is another example of a place for lingerie manufacturing in which so-called mountain girls make bras for global brands such as Zara and contribute significantly to the textile economy (BBC 2018). Times have changed, and so have consumer preferences.

In general, it is true that all the outfits showcased at fashion shows in Paris, Milan, London, and New York cannot be commercially viable to produce and market. But certain elements of the showcased fashions, such as color and material patterns, can be picked up by designers to influence future fashion clothing. Here are the seven predicted *fashion looks* for 2020: neon; buttery, colorful leather; big bags; tangerine; rose prints; disco collars; and rope belts and bucket hats (McIntosh 2020).

Conclusion

The purpose of the chapter was to discuss political fashion, eco fashion, ethnic fashion, and beachwear and underwear fashion. The section on political fashion includes who uses fashion to make political statements and how it is branded. Eco fashion related to the environment, whereas ethnic fashion was discussed in the context of gender and education and its impact on ethnic fashion. In the beachwear and underwear section, the impact of seasonality, age, and post-feminism on marketing strategy was also discussed.

Experiential Learning

1. List ten world leaders who used fashion as branding for their personality and communications. Write the associated messages and the marketing tools they used for their branding.
2. Discuss ten global brands that use the concept of eco fashion and the challenges associated with such a fashion orientation.
3. Compare and contrast marketing strategies of beachwear and underwear on each continent. Use your own comparative indicators with justification.

References

Aaronson, B. 1970. Some affective stereotypes of color. *International Journal of Symbology*, 2, 15–27.

Akou, H.M. 2007. Building a new world fashion: Islamic dress in the twenty-first century. *Fashion Theory*, 11(4), 403.

Allaire, C. 2018. How 6 indigenous designers are using fashion to reclaim their culture. May 31. www.vogue.com/article/indigenous-fashion-designers-cultural-appropriation-activism [Accessed on July 2, 2020].

Amy-Chinn, D. 2006. This is just for me(n): How the regulation of post-feminist lingerie advertising perpetuates women as object. *Journal of Consumer Culture*, 6(2), 155–175.

Angelis, A.D. 2013. Global swimwear market driven by the popularity of swimming. https://uk.finance.yahoo.com/news/global-swimwear-market-driven-popularity [Accessed on July 2, 2020].

Assmann, S. 2008. Between tradition and innovation: The Reinvention of the Kimono in Japanese consumer culture. *Fashion Theory: The Journal of Dress, Body & Culture*, 12(3), 359–376.

Bansal, P. 2008. *Elements of fashion and apparel designing*. Jaipur: Book Enclave.

BBC. 2018. The mountain girls making bras for Europe's chests. www.bbc.com/news/stories-45097050 [Accessed on July 2, 2020].

Bendell, J. & Kleanthous, A. 2007. Deeper luxury. www.wwf.org.uk/deeperluxury [Accessed on July 2, 2020].

Bigi, A., Treen, E. & Bal, A. 2016. How customer and product orientations shape political brands. *The Journal of Product and Brand Management*, 25(4), 365–372.

Bochner, S. 1994. Cross-cultural differences in the self-concept: A test of Hofstede's individualism/collectivism distinction. *Journal of Cross-Cultural Psychology*, June, 273–283.

Bruce, M. & Daly, L. 2006. Buyer behaviour for fast fashion. *Journal of Fashion Marketing and Management*, 10(3), 329–344.

Buckley, C. & Clark, H. 2012. Conceptualizing fashion in everyday lives. *Design Issues*, 28(4), 18–28.

Cardona, F.J. & Rabolt, N.J. 1997. Contemporary outer dress and clothing market source use of Middle Eastern women. *Journal of Consumer Studies and Home Economics*, 21(1), 55–74.

Cervellon, M.C. & Shammas, L. 2013. The value of sustainable luxury in mature markets: A customer-based approach. *Journal of Corporate Citizenship*, 52(52), 90–101.

Chan, T.Y. & Wong, C. 2012. The consumption side of sustainable fashion supply chain: Understanding fashion consumer eco-fashion consumption decision. *Journal of Fashion Marketing and Management*, 16(2), 193–215.

Chang, W. 1990. The study of Korean fashion trend color system. Master Thesis. Iwha Women's University, Seoul.

Chibnik, M., Colloredo-Mansfeld, R., Lee, M., Milgram, B.L., Rovine, V. & Weil, J. 2004. Artists and aesthetics: Case studies of creativity in the ethnic arts market. *Anthropology of Work Review*, 25(1–2), 3–8.

Choi, M., Shim, Y. & Syn, H. 2006. Comparison on color preference of BRICs Consumers. *Journal of Korean Society Costume*, 56, 118–131.

Clarke, T. & Costall, A. 2008. The emotional connotations of color: A qualitative investigation. *Color Research Application*, 33, 406–410.

Davis, E. 2009. Engineering swimwear. *The Journal of the Textile Institute*, 32–36.

Delgado, H. 2018. When fashion becomes a political statement. www.cnn.com/style/article/fashion-influence-politics-and-culture/index.html [Accessed on July 2, 2020].

Deng, X., Hui, S.K. & Hutchinson, J.W. 2010. Consumer preferences for color combinations: An empirical analysis of similarity-based relationships. *Journal of Consumer Psychology*, *20*, 476–484.

Doran, K.B. 2002. Lessons learned in cross-cultural research of Chinese and North American consumers. *Journal of Business Research*, *55*(October), 823–829.

Easey, M. 2009. *Fashion marketing*. Oxford: Wiley-Blackwell.

Eckersley, M. 2004. Joining people & brands. *Design Management Review*, *15*(3), 60–63.

Edwards, T. 2018. Living dolls? The role of clothing and fashion in 'sexualisation'. *Sexualities*.

EMF. 2017. Ellen MacArthur Foundation: A new textiles economy: Redesigning fashion's future. www.ellenmacarthurfoundation.org/assets/downloads/A-New-Textiles-Economy_Summary-of-Findings_Updated_1-12-17.pdf [Accessed on July 2, 2020].

Esty, D. & Winston, A. 2006. *Green to gold: How smart companies use environmental strategy to innovate, create value, and build competitive advantage*. New Haven, CT: Yale University Press.

Eunyoung, J. 2007. The study on the international analysis of color sensibility and fashion color preference according to Korean personal color. Doctoral Thesis. Catholic University, Daegu.

Fihlani, P. 2016. How South African women are reclaiming the headscarf. www.bbc.com/news/world-africa-36461213 [Accessed on July 2, 2020].

Fraser, T. & Banks, A. 2004. *Designer's color manual: The complete guide to color theory and application*. San Francisco: Chronicle Books.

Friedman, V. 2016. When politics became a fashion statement. www.nytimes.com/2016/12/13/fashion/the-year-in-style-politics-dressing.html [Accessed on July 2, 2020].

Gabrielli, V., Baghi, I. & Codeluppi, V. 2013. Consumption practices of fast fashion products: A consumer-based approach. *Journal of Fashion Marketing and Management*, *17*(2), 206–224.

Gerretsen, I. & Kottasova, I. 2020. The world is paying high price for cheap clothes. www.cnn.com/2020/05/03/business/cheap-clothing-fast-fashion-climate-change-intl/index.html [Accessed on July 2, 2020].

GIA. 2020. Global Industry Analysts Inc. swimwear and beachwear: A global strategic business report. www.strategyr.com/market-report-swimwear-and-beachwear-forecasts-global-industry-analysts-inc.asp [Accessed July 2, 2020].

Gibson, P. & Seibold, S. 2014. Understanding and influencing eco-luxury consumers. *International Journal of Social Economics*, *41*(9), 780–800.

Guardian. 2015. Lingerie capital of feels the pinch as recession deepens. www.theguardian.com/world/2015/jul/26/lingerie-capital-brazil-recession-deepens [Accessed on July 2, 2020].

Gustafson, K. 2015. Victoria's Secret debuts $2M fantasy bra. www.cnbc.com/2015/11/02/victorias-secret-debuts-2m-fantasy-bra.html [Accessed on July 2, 2020].

Halasa, M. & Salam, R. 2008. *The secret life of Syrian lingerie: Intimacy and Design*. San Francisco, USA: Chronical books.

Hall, E.T. 1976. *Beyond culture*. New York: Doubleday.

Hatton, C. 2016. Why Chinese officials are afraid to look too smart. www.bbc.com/news/magazine-35775958 [Accessed on July 2, 2020].

Heather, K. & Weber, J.M. 2012. A look at gender differences and marketing implications. *International Journal of Business and Social Science*, 3(21), 247–253.

Hirscher, A. & Niinimaki, K. 2013. Fashion activism through participatory design. European Academy of Design Conference, Gothenburg University, Sweden.

Hofstede, G. 2001. *Culture's consequences: Comparing values, behaviors, institutions, and organizations across nations.* Thousand Oaks, CA: Sage Publications.

Howlett, N., Pine, K., Orakçioglu, I. & Fletcher, B. 2013. The influence of clothing on first impressions. *Journal of Fashion Marketing and Management*, 17(1), 38–48.

Hsu, H.J. & Burns, L.D. 2012. The effect of culture, long- term orientation, and gender on consumers' perceptions of clothing values. *Social Behavior and Personality*, 40(10), 1585–1595.

Jackson, D. 2008. Selling politics: The impact of celebrities' political beliefs on young Americans. *Journal of Political Marketing*, 6(4), 67–83.

Joyce, E. 2018. Does bralet boom spell the end of high-rise boobs? www.bbc.com/news/45572001 [Accessed on July 2, 2020].

Kauppinen-Raisanen, H. & Luomala, H.T. 2010. Exploring consumers' product-specific colour meanings. *Qualitative Market Research*, 13(3), 287–308.

Kelly, M. 2010. Clothes, culture, and context: Female dress in Kuwait. *Fashion Theory: The Journal of Dress, Body & Culture*, 14(2), 215–236.

Khaire, M. 2011. The Indian fashion industry and traditional Indian crafts. *Business History Review*, 85(2), 345–366.

Kim, H., Ho, J.C. & Yoon, N. 2013. The motivational drivers of fast fashion avoidance. *Journal of Fashion Marketing and Management*, 17(2), 243–260.

La Monica, P.R. 2019. Time may be running out for Victoria's Secret. www.cnn.com/2019/07/15/investing/victorias-secret-l-brands/index.html.

Lea-Greenwood, G. 2013. *Fashion marketing communications*. West Sussex: Wiley & Sons.

Lee, A. 2020. Congressional democrats criticized for wearing Kente cloth at event honoring George Floyd. www.cnn.com/2020/06/08/politics/democrats-criticized-kente-cloth-trnd/index.html [Accessed on July 2, 2020].

Lee, E.J., Fairhurst, A. & Dillard, S. 2002. Usefulness of ethnicity in international consumer marketing. *Journal of International Consumer Marketing*, 14(4), 25–48.

Leitch, V. 1996. Costly compensations: Postmodern fashion, politics, identity. *Modern Fiction Studies*, 42(1), 111–128.

Mahnke, F.H. 1996. *Color, environment, and human response*. New York: Reinhold.

Marci, K. 2020. The lingerie market explained in 7 charts. https://edited.com/resources/lingerie-market-2 [Accessed on July 2, 2020].

Mark, M. 2018. A Melania source explains the meaning behind the controversial 'I really don't care, do u?' jacket she wore on a trip to visit immigrant children. www.businessinsider.com.

McIntosh, S. 2020. Fashion lookahead: Seven major looks for 2020. www.bbc.com/news/entertainment-arts-50087110 [Accessed on July 2, 2020].

Meinhold, R. & Irons, J. 2013 A critical inquiry into fashion. In *Fashion myths: A cultural critique*. Bielefeld: Transcript Verlag.

Miller, J. 2005. Fashion and democratic relationships. *Polity*, 37(1), 3–23.

Mintel. 2004. *Underwear retailing*. London: Mintel.

Morimoto, M. & Chang, S. 2009. Western and Asian models in Japanese fashion magazine ads: The relationship with brand origins and international versus domestic magazines. *Journal of International Consumer Marketing, 21*(3), 173–187.

Naujoks, D. 2010. Diasporic identities: Reflections on transnational belonging. *Diasporic Studies, 3*(1), 1–21.

Niinimäki, K. 2010. Eco-clothing, consumer identity and ideology. *Sustainable Development, 18*(3), 150–162.

Nitse, P.S., Parker, K.R., Krumwiede, D. & Ottaway, T. 2004. The impact of color in the e-commerce marketing of fashions: An exploratory study. *European Journal of Marketing, 38*(7), 898–915.

Obukhova, E., Zuckerman, E. & Zhang, J. 2014. When politics froze fashion: The effect of the cultural revolution on naming in Beijing. *American Journal of Sociology, 120*(2), 555–583.

Poli, D.D. 1995. *Beachwear and bathing-costume.* Modena, Italy: Zanfi Editori.

Posner, H. 2011. *Marketing fashion.* London: Laurence King Pub.

Rapp, J. 2019. The designers changing the conversation around lingerie. www.cnn.com/style/article/lingerie-designers-inclusivity/index.html [Accessed on July 2, 2020].

Rovine, V.L. 2009. Colonialism's clothing: Africa, France, and the deployment of fashion. *Design Issues, 25*(3), 44–61.

Ruoh-Nan, Y., Karen, H.H. & LaVon, F.B. 2012. Marketing eco-fashion: The Influence of brand name and message explicitness. *Journal of Marketing Communications, 18*(2), 151–168.

Sadof, K. 2017. Finding a visual voice: The #Euromaidan impact on Ukrainian instagram users. In U. Frömming, S. Köhn, S. Fox, & M. Terry (Eds.), *Digital environments: Ethnographic perspectives across global online and offline spaces* (pp. 239–250). Bielefeld: Transcript Verlag.

Sawer, M. 2007. Wearing your politics on your sleeve: The role of political colours in social movements. *Social Movement Studies, 6*(1), 39–56.

Shin, S.H. & Cynthia, L.I. 2007. The importance of understanding the shape of diverse ethnic female consumers for developing jeans sizing systems. *International Journal of Consumer Studies, 31*(2), 135–143.

SMC. 2018. Organic cotton. StellaMcCartney.com [Accessed on July 2, 2020].

Smith, N. 2018. North Korean fashion police crackdown on banned haircuts. www.telegraph.co.uk/news/2018/08/17/north-korean-fashion-police-crack-banned-haircuts/ [Accessed on July 2, 2020].

Sproles, G.B. 1981. Analyzing fashion life cycles: Principles and perspectives. *Journal of Marketing, 45*(4), 116–124.

Stephens, N. 1991. Cognitive age: A useful concept for advertising. *Journal of Advertising, 20*(4), 37–48.

Strübel, J. 2012. Get your Gele: Nigerian dress, diasporic identity, and translocalism. *Journal of Pan African Studies, 4*(9), 24–41.

Tan, R. 2017. Politics' influence on fashion is greater than you think. www.elle.sg/fashion/trends/politics-influence-on-fashion-is-greater-than-you-think-7129070 [Accessed on July 2, 2020].

Thucydides. 2017. *History of the Peloponnesian War.* New York: Courier Corporation.

Vrontis, D. & Vronti, P. 2004. Levi Strauss: An international marketing investigation. *Journal of Fashion Marketing and Management, 8,* 389.

Wilson, J.P. 2015. The triple bottom line. *International Journal of Retail & Distribution Management, 43*(4), 432–447.

Won, S. & Westland, S. 2016. Colour meaning and context. *Color Research & Application*, 42(4), 450–459.

Wright, A. 1988. *The beginner's guide to colour psychology*. London: Colour Affects Ltd.

Yangzom, D. 2016. Clothing and social movements: Tibet and the politics of dress. *Social Movement Studies*, 15(6), 622–633.

Yu, H.L., Kim, C., Lee, J. & Hong, N. 2001. An analysis of modern fashion designs as influenced by Asian ethnic dress. *Journal of Consumer Studies and Home Economics*, 25(4), 309–321.

8 Fad, Fashion, and the Indian Consumer

Introduction

India witnesses a rise in fashion activities with the growth of its economy (Bellman & Passariello 2007). Although the fashion industry continues to be the source of much attention to academics and practitioners (Akehurst & Alexander 1996; Vida & Fairhurst 1998), the decision-making process of Indian consumers relating to fashion consumption appears to be an under-developed issue in the extant literature. The majority of previous studies has focused on internationalization (Fernie, Moore, & Lawrie 1998; Moore 1997), market entry (Sarkar & Cavusgil 1996), manufacturing (Driscoll & Paliwoda 1997; Hill, Hwang, & Kim 1990), and the service sector (Erramilli 1991; Erramilli & Rao 1990). Limited attention has been devoted to the development of the fashion industry in India and to factors that contribute to the decision-making process in the Indian context. The reason for the gap may be that until recently India was a developing country and fashion consumption was relatively too expensive for ordinary citizens. However, the new Indian market economy has boosted the quality of life in general, which has created a demand for fashion goods. Therefore, the purpose of the chapter is to identify factors that impact the decision-making process of Indian consumers in the context of fad and fashion.

The term *fad* refers to a fashion that becomes popular in a culture relatively quickly but loses popularity fairly quickly as well. Some fads reappear when the next generation discovers the old fashion. As a result, marketers target youth to become brand savvy and fad obsessive, changing their attitudes from one fad to another. For example, fads from past generations are increasingly becoming popular as teens dig through their parents' closets to find the latest fashions. The popularity of tights with big belts, long sweaters, and skinny jeans manifest the trend. Parents realize that they have something in common with their children in what they believe was cool and in style. The styles—embellishments, prints, and colors—have become staples and constantly revisited by designers. The rage for "gypsy" and bohemian chic and silhouettes, such as long tunics and peasant dresses, is another reinvention of hippie chic that goes back at least 60 years. The ethnic-inspired look has become almost a classic fashion niche; that is, the best of Indian embellishment is being combined with highly wearable Western styles (Williamson 2005). Clearly, the style does not fade but evolves.

Fads have a profound effect on young consumers and their purchase decisions, as they are attuned to brand recognition and able to identify themselves with fads. If a celebrity is seen wearing something that looks *cool*, everyone wants to wear the same thing until the next *cool* thing comes into style. Especially with the change of seasons, a change in fads is witnessed. In summer, blonde hair may be the *in* color, but when fall rolls around auburn may be the color that turns heads. Marketing managers realize that the short-term nature of fads has a relative strength in its flexibility (Lilly & Tammy 2003). Having knowledge about fad adds value to product development and contributes to future planning and sales targets.

On the other hand, fashion is a form of imitation and social equalization (Simmel 1957). It changes incessantly and differentiates one from another, and one social stratum from another. Fashion unites similar social classes by using objects such as clothing, jewelry, and cosmetics (Eicher & Sumberg 1995). Dress is much more than protecting the body; it is a form of differentiation within a group. Fashion and consumption behavior are influenced by social norms and values (Back 1985). Based on a literature survey, this chapter identifies the influence of five factors—Indian consumers, Indian apparel and fashion, economy, culture, and media and films—on the decision-making process for fashion products.

Indian Consumers

The number of Indian consumers has grown recently, leading to a surge in the purchase of luxury, designer goods, and fashion brands. Because of the economic boom and overseas expansion, India has developed a new class of consumers with more money and an interest in global brands (Bellman & Passariello 2007). Economic growth is another factor for increased disposable income and a new lavish lifestyle (Upadhyay 2007). Indian consumers are sophisticated and savvy and embrace brands to express values and communication styles that focus on collective hierarchy (Nelson & Devanathan 2006). The enticement towards premium brands is due to the exclusivity and prestige associated with them (Commuri 2009). Emerging markets are conscious of fashion brands, predominantly by youths. In an attempt to understand the determinants of fashion clothing involvement of Indian youth, Khare and Rakesh (2010) identified that Indian youth were involved with all four dimensions of branded fashion wear—consumption, product, advertising, and purchase decision—and that no significant differences existed between males and females on fashion wear.

International clothing retailers are the key drivers for globalization of the clothing industry (Gereffi 2005). The West has significantly influenced India. As the economy progressed, the need for Western items such as fashion increased. For example, when the magazines *Vogue* (American) and

Vogue India are placed next to each other, they appear to be very similar. The text and headlines are very alike. The magazines differ in that models featured in *Vogue India* are of Indian decent, whereas models seen in *Vogue* usually resemble an American Caucasian woman (Smith 2011).

Indian Apparel and Fashion

Indian apparel plays a historic role in Indian society. It has been important in establishing, maintaining, and altering the image of different social groups or castes. In fact, each caste may have its own distinctive form of dress (Tarlo 1993). Indians may adopt Western clothes to escape the stringent and debilitating marks of caste identity (Subbaraman 1999). It neutralizes inequality in social class. Interestingly enough, when villagers reject ethnic wear, the cosmopolitan elite readopt traditional wear (Mondal 1999). Western wear became a medium for social advancement for the lower class, whereas ethnic wear, especially for women, was used to achieve a distinct cultural identity. Thus, ethnic wear needed to be customized to suit the growing affluent, cosmopolitan, upper-middle class. The Indian diaspora uses ethnic wear substantially for special occasions and in specific situations when a group of individuals meets with others who share similar traditions. A total of 38 percent of Indians claim that special occasions drive most apparel purchases, compared with 6 percent of Chinese and 3 percent of Russians (Gangopadhyay 2007). Indians have been able to maintain distinct traditions of dress, an exquisite cuisine, and indigenous forms of artistic expression in a way that others may not. Ethnic wear is an important aspect in India, but the degree to which ethnic wear affects the perception of social class varies dramatically across regions. It is also found that ethnic wear, innovation in style, and opinion leaders are correlated (Chakrabarti & Baisya 2009).

Economy

India's GDP growth rate has been approximately 9 percent in recent years, partly because of the increase in globalization and outsourcing. India is one of the largest economies in terms of purchasing power parity. More than 200 Fortune firms operate in India (Johnson & Tellis 2008). More than one million Indians are believed to have liquid wealth of at least $100k (Upadhyay 2007). Thus, India's economic growth has a strong impact on the purchasing power and behavior of Indian consumers. Although India has typically been thought of as a traditional country in terms of fashion, recently there has been a shift to a more modern India, which is attributed to Western influence on Indians, particularly youths. It is the prevalence of Western culture that is a strong contributor to changing Indian consumer behavior. Western products appear in India as a result of the country's economic development and need for the status that comes with certain material items. This phenomenon has occurred before in countries such as France, with the bourgeoisie culture.

A middle class emerged, and the need for high-status goods became a reality because of economic development (Miller 1981).

India is one of the world's major exporters of apparel and textiles, particularly high-quality silk and high-end clothing labels, rivaling global luxury brands such as Prada or Gucci. One third of India's exports are fabrics such as cotton, jute, silk, and wool. Production of these fabrics accounts for the employment of 35 million Indians (Bremner & Lakshman 2007). India's exports of apparel and textiles globally are worth more than $20b (Commuri 2009). In the 1980s, apparel exports only accounted for $600m, but the amount grew more than 15 times, an indication of a steady export growth. Because of the growth, the Indian government gave upscale retailers a boost by allowing foreign companies to own a controlling interest of 51 percent in joint ventures operating single-brand stores (Narayan & Carsen 2006).

Culture

Culture is the knowledge, language, values, customs, and material objects that are passed from person to person and from one generation to the next in a human group or society (Freeburg & Workman 2008). Cultural values are important in international marketing and personal values in determining consumer behavior (Ghanem & Kalliny 2009). The term *values* is defined as a centrally held enduring belief, which guides actions and judgments across specific situations and beyond immediate goals to more ultimate end-states of existence. As values are internalized, they become unconscious and conscious criteria for guiding behavior. Indian consumers adopt global brands as a symbol of global values systems to express their values and beliefs through their shopping habits. Fashion reflects underlying cultural categories, which correspond to the basic ways we characterize the world (Shoham 2002). Thus, culture distinguishes between what is appropriate at different times and contexts, and for different genders and ages. Such differences help fashion designers become creative, globally.

Dress norms vary, with different aspects of norms (Meier 1982; Workman & Freeburg 2000). India is a diverse country with 29 states and seven union territories, each having its own distinct culture, unique beliefs, and different religions—Hinduism, Muslim, Christianity, Sikhs, and Jews. Given the diverse Indian culture and strong religious views, it is important to discuss its effects on fashion in India. Cultural values stem from different levels such as individual, organizational, and national. Because of the changing and growing structure of the Indian population, an individual may be influenced by any of these values. India has traditionally been strict about the clothing its citizens wear, especially for women who wear a *sari*—a cloth folded and draped on the body. In Kerala, Hindu women believe sleeveless sari blouses and Western dresses are immoral (Osella & Osella 2007). Saris have been a long-time expression of cultural identity in India. Because the aspects of dress norms are interrelated, the process of social control is complex.

The Indian dress such as sari may decrease in popularity because of Western influence (Hansen 2004). Thus, fashion designers combine Indian motifs with Western styles in Bollywood films in an effort to reach a global audience, and thus culture conversely attempts to affect Western culture (Bremner & Lakshman 2007). Western clothing such as European-style skirts, trousers, or T-shirts may still be considered inappropriate for formal or semi-formal occasions, yet male Indians are known to wear Western-style suits for business purposes. This shows an approval for some styles of Western clothing but disapproval for others.

However, there has been a shift towards a more Westernized type of clothing. With the influence of Western culture in India, the country is moving to combine Eastern and Western types of apparel. Fashionable ethnic wear has been on the rise to retain the Indian tradition while incorporating Western design. This type of dress is popular among the younger generations who wish to balance tradition with modernity (Chakrabarti & Baisya 2009). This opens up a new market for fashion retailers, who are looking for opportunities to cater to a modern yet traditional demographic.

Media and Films

With technological advancements, media and communications have enabled people—even in the most isolated places—to absorb the culture of others and gain information about the latest products, features, and brands (Pimblett & Whitelock 1997). Media have a unique ability to reach and influence consumers. In this chapter, media relates to the Indian Bollywood film industry and TV. Bollywood is a popular Indian film industry, which has the power to influence consumers considerably. Bollywood influences fashion in two ways: (1) the projection of brand images and styles shown in the movies and (2) the promotion of fashions by celebrities. It is not a secret that Bollywood film producers accept incentives from international advertisers to promote their brands in the films. High-end brand names are known to appear in Bollywood films such as Tommy Hilfiger or Ralph Lauren Polo. This product placement by international advertisers is a strategic move because of the long length of Bollywood films—usually three hours, with an intermission break of about ten minutes—and because of the high interest and reach of the films (Nelson & Devanathan 2006). The more consumers see the Western style in media, the more likely they are to imitate the trend. In fact, much of India's fashion consumption is directly dependent on what goes on in feature films and the film industry (Venkatesh 1994).

Another Bollywood influence on fashion relates to celebrity influence. Quite often, Bollywood celebrities wear or promote high-end fashion brands. For instance, Shahrukh Khan, one of Bollywood's biggest stars, is *brand ambassador* for Tag Heuer watches, a high-end brand in the watch industry (Bellman & Passariello 2007). Fans and viewers of Bollywood films tend to imitate these celebrities if they are portrayed as idols, similar to Western culture. In addition to seeing celebrities switching to high-fashion Westernized clothing—both in movies and in public for big events—consumers watch TV and read fashion magazines, keeping them abreast of the latest trends and products in fashion. Consumer affluence is also directly related to media influence. With the increasing amount of disposable income, consumers not only purchase luxury goods and high-end fashion items, but also accessories such as TVs and computers. This allows even a greater reach for media to affect Indian consumers. TV, satellite, and cable are other mediums responsible for the dissemination of fashion to Indian consumers.

Further, the intermingling of Indian and Western values has led Indians to adopt global brands. Because of its reach and availability, TV plays a major role in the adoption process. TV reaches across India as no other technology has done in the country's history (Venkatesh 1994). Furthermore, media are present in 65 percent of India's rural and urban areas, attributing to the increased acceptance of Western styles (Nelson & Devanathan 2006). Consumer behavior significantly influences the fashion industry in India. Cloth purchasing is a high-involvement activity for most Indian consumers. The youth population—Y generation—has grown up in a post-economic, liberalized country and has different patterns of behavior from past generations. With political liberalization, Western brands were brought to Indian consumers, introducing the Western wear and lifestyle. There is a growing market for fashion products in India, as Indian consumers associate Western brands with status symbol, better quality of life, and enhancement of self-image (Khare & Rakesh 2010).

Decision-Making Process

The consumer decision-making process is a complex phenomenon. So, it is important that products fit into the world of the consumer (Pimblett & Whitelock 1997). India has begun to adopt the new fashion culture with respect to high-end apparel. The transformation of the middle class has played a significant role in changing the consumption fashion pattern of Indians. This transformation can be attributed to developments in the manufacturing and services sectors as a result of multinational corporations' investments in these sectors. As the new middle-class population acquires more income through savings and through the introduction of the credit system, coupled with the development of the luxury shopping environment and outlets, it provides Indian consumers with opportunities to consume more fashion-related products. The proliferation of the mainstream media has played a significant role in increasing fashion consumption in India.

India demonstrates high levels of materialistic values that are related to spirituality (Lindridge & Dibb 2003). For most Indians, possessions indicate happiness and well-being, and wealth is believed to be bestowed from compliance with religious rituals. Fashion clothing may be seen as a status symbol not only for the individual, but also for the family and social groups. The high growth rate in retail is driven by enhanced purchasing power, increased urbanization, high awareness, intense competition, changing lifestyle, and large number of youth (Narang 2009). About half of the youth population of India is fashion conscious and would like to try new things. They would like a great deal of variety in their lives and want to learn about art, culture, and history (Williamson 2005). It is their lifestyle and consumer behavior that dictates what happens to the Indian fashion industry.

Indians have an upward social mobility tendency because of the creation of more skilled and unskilled jobs. Indian labor laws and regulations have a rigid wage system for the two categories, and a high elasticity in supply of labor exists. That is, a slight change in wage rate attracts a greater supply of labor to the workforce. In other words, as there is a narrow gap between skilled and unskilled labor in terms of wages, there is pressure to be perceived differently, causing the skilled labor force to engage in the consumption of luxury products to acclaim the prestige associated with skilled workers. It is all about perception and image. The high rate of educated women in society and a thriving service sector that employs predominantly women have systemically created a demand for luxury fashion and products. An indication of these phenomena can be seen in the role women play in society, labor participation, and the changing structure of the family (Venkatesh 1994).

Marketing Strategy

Several global companies have now realized that India is a potential market for fashion. Although the limited exposure of Indian youth to global fashion clothing brands and the lack of branded stock in India's stores may limit the fashion industry's growth, factors such as brand consciousness, modern lifestyle, influence of Western culture, frequent international trips, and increased levels of education and disposable income have led India to become one of the top three most brand-conscious countries in the world (Bhardwaj, Park, & Kim 2011). Actually, Indians are aware of the global brands they want but are unable to purchase them because of the unavailability of all brands in India. Indian families and groups use fashion as a status symbol and self-image. Global brands do incorporate global images in their products and promotion strategies to convince brand-conscious Indian consumers to purchase their brands. This strategy is effective as Indians want to enhance their self-image and establish their membership with their counterparts in developed countries. Marketing practices and channels of distribution structure reflect the level of economic development and the socio-cultural dimensions of a country (Ahmed & Al-Motawa 1997). Managers need to recognize that not only developed nations can influence India, but also that it can be the other way around. Clearly, developed nations are interested in conducting businesses in India to develop competitive advantage and be globally competitive. Indian fashion managers should do the same.

Conclusion

Indian fashion is influenced by Western fashion and global fashion brands. It is important to understand that culture impacts every aspect of a society, including the thinking and acting of every member of a group. Cultural values are important variables in international advertising (Ghanem & Kalliny 2009). The emergence of luxury fashion has boosted local designers' work, which is now being featured in global fashion magazines such as *Vanity Fair*. Anamika Khanna and Manish Arora are the first Indian designers to be invited to showcase their work at the Paris Fashion Week (Bremner & Lakshman 2007).

Products are not seen as physical objects but as bundles of consumer benefits; thus, creating a distinction between product and brand is imperative (Pimblett & Whitelock 1997). Fashion promotes these benefits. Although marketers use national boundaries as a guide for adaption, it is not always effective, because consumer preferences vary greatly within and among countries. For example, personal values affect consumers' judgments, preferences, and choices. Values may be related to exposure to mass media, preferences for television programs, and preferences for fashion products. Consequently, values have been used for segmentation, product planning, and promotion decisions. Because of these cultural and fashion preference differences, marketers should take these differences into consideration (McCarty & Hattwick 1992). In general, Indians put a greater emphasis on quality-price match than just brand names (Kawazu & Ishizaka 2012).

Another important element of fashion is color. Colors are controversial but play an integral role in fashion. Different cultures interpret color in different ways. Therefore, it is important that unfavorable colors are excluded in both clothing and advertising. Products fail because of symbolic meaning attached to certain colors. Some feel that human responses to colors are stable, therefore applicable to everyone, whereas others disagree, asserting that responses and preferences to colors carry across culture, gender, and age, among others (Singh 2006). A safe color across many cultures is blue, because it is often perceived positively. Because India has a significant Muslim population, green is a good color to use as it is considered a sacred color in that population. A study relating to color interpretation in India and its impact on fashion is worth pursuing.

Experiential Learning

1. Explore five reasons why Indian luxury may be perceived superior to Western luxury, as evidenced by many Western luxury brands' inability to make significant inroads in Indian luxury markets.
2. Compare North Indian and South Indian fashion, style, and preferences. Use your own comparative indicators with justification.
3. Search for five reasons why Indian women love gold more than pearls as fashion accessories. Explore and explain in the context of national, economic, and culture issues.

References

Ahmed, A.A. & Al-Motawa, A.A. 1997. Communication and related channel phenomena in international markets: The Saudi car market. *Journal of Global Marketing*, *10*(3), 67–82.

Akehurst, G. & Alexander, N. 1996. *The internationalization of retailing*. Oxon: Frank Cass.

Back, K.W. 1985. *Modernism and fashion: A social psychological interpretation: The psychology of fashion*. M. Solomon (Ed.). Lexington, MA: Lexington Books, 3–14.

Bellman, E. & Passariello, C. 2007. As economy grows, India goes for designer goods. *Wall Street Journal*, *249*(71), A1–A17.

Bhardwaj, V., Park, H. & Kim, Y. 2011. The effect of Indian consumers' life satisfaction on brand behavior toward a U.S. global brand. *Journal of International Consumer Marketing*, *23*(2), 105–116.

Bremner, B. & Lakshman, N. 2007. India craves the catwalk. *Business Week Online*, *4*(5), 18.

Chakrabarti, S. & Baisya, R. 2009. The influences of consumer innovativeness and consumer evaluation attributes in the purchase of fashionable ethnic wear in India. *International Journal of Consumer Studies*, *33*(6), 706–714.

Commuri, S. 2009. The impact of counterfeiting on genuine-item consumers' brand relationships. *Journal of Marketing*, *73*(3), 86–98.

Driscoll, A.M. & Paliwoda, S.J. 1997. Dimensionalizing international market entry mode choice. *Journal of Marketing Management*, *13*(2–4), 57–87.

Eicher, J. & Sumberg, B. 1995. World fashion, ethnic and national dress. In B. Sumburg (Ed.), *Dress and ethnicity: Change across space and time* (pp. 295–307). Washington, DC: Oxford.

Erramilli, M.K. 1991. The experience factor in foreign market entry behavior of service firms. *Journal of International Business Studies*, *22*(3), 479–501.

Erramilli, M.K. & Rao, C.P. 1990. Choice of foreign market entry modes by service firms: Role of market knowledge. *Management International Review*, *30*(2), 135–150.

Fernie, J., Moore, C.M. & Lawrie, A. 1998. A tale of two cities: An examination of fashion designer retailing within London and New York. *Journal of Product and Brand Management*, *7*(5), 366–378.

Freeburg, B. & Workman, J. 2008. *Dress and society*. New York: Fairchild Books and Visuals.

Gangopadhyay, K. 2007. The great Indian bazaar. *India International Centre Quarterly*, *34*(2), 152–169.

Gereffi, G. 2005. The global economy: Organization, governance, and development. In N.J. Smelser and R. Swedverg (Eds.), *Handbook of economic sociology* (pp. 160–182). Princeton, NJ: Princeton University Press and Russell Sage Foundation.

Ghanem, S. & Kalliny, M. 2009. The role of the advertising agency in the cultural message content of advertisements: A comparison of the Middle East and United States. *Journal of Global Marketing*, *22*(4), 313–328.

Hansen, K.T. 2004. The world in dress: Anthropological perspectives on clothing, fashion and culture. *Annual Review of Anthropology*, *33*, 369–392.

Hill, C.W.L., Hwang, P. & Kim, W.C. 1990. An eclectic theory of the choice of international entry mode. *Strategic Management Journal*, *11*(2), 117–128.

Johnson, J. & Tellis, G. 2008. Drivers of success for market entry into China and India. *Journal of Marketing*, 72(May), 1.

Kawazu, N. & Ishizaka, E. 2012. Marketing strategies targeting the middle rich in India. *Journal of Marketing & Communication*, 7(3), 4–15.

Khare, A. & Rakesh, S. 2010. Predictors of fashion clothing involvement among Indian youth. *Journal of Targeting, Measurement & Analysis for Marketing*, 18(3), 209–220.

Lilly, B. & Tammy, N.R. 2003. Fads: Segmenting the fad-buyer market. *Journal of Consumer Marketing*, 20(3), 252–265.

Lindridge, A. & Dibb, S. 2003. Is culture' a justifiable variable for market segmentation? A cross-cultural example. *Journal of Consumer Behaviour*, 2(3), 269–286.

McCarty, J. & Hattwick, P. 1992. Cultural value orientations: A comparison of magazine advertisements from the United States and Mexico. In J.F. Sherry, Jr. & B. Sternthal (Eds.), *Advances in Consumer Research Volume 19* (pp. 34–38). Provo, UT: Association for Consumer Research.

Meier, R. 1982. Perspectives on the concept of social control. In R.H. Turner & J.F. Short (Eds.), *Annual Review of Sociology* (pp. 35–55). Palo Alto, CA: Annual Reviews, Inc.

Miller, M.B. 1981. *The Bon Marché: Bourgeois culture and the department store, 1869–1920*. Princeton, NJ: Princeton University Press.

Mondal, A. 1999. Clothing matters: Dress and identity in India. *Interventions London*, 1, 621–622.

Moore, C.M. 1997. La mode sans frontiers: The internationalization of fashion retailing. *Journal of Fashion Marketing and Management*, 1(4), 345–356.

Narang, R. 2009. Profile of young India and its implications for modern retailing. *Retail Digest*, 30–33.

Narayan, S. & Carsen, J. 2006. India's lust for luxe. *Time International* (South Pacific Edition), April 10, 36(3).

Nelson, M.R. & Devanathan, N. 2006. Brand placement Bollywood style. *Journal of Consumer Behavior*, 5(3), 211–221.

Osella, C. & Osella, F. 2007. Muslim style in South India. *Fashion Theory: The Journal of Dress, Body & Culture*, 11(2), 233–252.

Pimblett, C. & Whitelock, J. 1997. The Standardization debate in international marketing. *Journal of Global Marketing*, 10(3), 45–66.

Sarkar, M. & Cavusgil, T. 1996. Trends in international business thought: A review of international market entry mode research: Integration and synthesis. *The International Executive*, 38(6), 835–847.

Shoham, A. 2002. Determinants of fashion attributes importance: An Israeli study. *Journal of International Consumer Marketing*, 15(2), 43–61.

Simmel, G. 1957. Fashion. *The American Journal of Sociology*, 62(6), 541–558.

Singh, S. 2006. Impact of color on marketing. *Management Decision*, 44(6), 783–789.

Smith, V. 2011. Vogue fashion, features, and more. *Vogue.com* [Accesses on July 2, 2020].

Subbaraman, S. 1999. Cataloging ethnicity interventions. *International Journal of Postcolonial Studies*, 1(4), 572–589.

Tarlo, E. 1993. *Clothing matters: Dress and identity in India*. Chicago, IL: University of Chicago Press, 141.

Upadhyay, R. 2007. Retailing's rapid rise in India. *WWD: Women's Wear Daily*, 193(38), 2.

Venkatesh, A. 1994. India's changing consumer economy: A cultural perspective. *Advances in Consumer Research*, 21(1), 323–332.

Vida, I. & Fairhurst, A. 1998. International expansion of retail firms: A theoretical approach for future investigations. *Journal of Retailing and Consumer Services,* 5(3), 143–151.

Williamson, R. 2005. From Boho to Beading: India draws designers with exotic inspirations. *WWD: Women's Wear Daily, 189,* 1–9.

Workman, J.E. & Freeburg, E.W. 2000. Testing the expanded definition of the normative order. *Clothing and Textiles Research Journal,* 18(2), 90–99.

Part III

Cases on Emerging Luxury Markets

9 Colombia

Decision-Making Process

Luxury brands are one of the most profitable and fastest-growing segments of luxury (Berthon, Pitt, Parent, & Berthon 2009). Global brands have business goals in emerging markets to gain market share in the rapidly growing global economies (Kumar, Sharma, Shah, & Rajan 2013). Purchase decisions of consumers in emerging markets are heavily influenced by recommendations from friends and family members (Atsmon, Kuentz, & Seong 2012). Social aspects (e.g. status and how others perceive the purchases) and price (compared with functionality and quality of the goods) has a great influence on the purchase of luxury goods (Shukla 2012). Older consumers tend to prefer local products and a desire to fit in society based on how others will perceive their purchases (Lee, Klobas, Tezinde, & Murphy 2010). By identifying luxury preferences of individuals in emerging markets such as Colombia, luxury brands can develop a competitive advantage by deploying marketing capabilities (Kaufmann & Roesch 2012). Some argue that luxury brands have an *imperialist mindset* to sell existing products to established upscale markets in emerging economies (London & Hart 2004).

Online Marketing

Online marketing can take many forms—websites, pop-ups, and social media. A major challenge lies in creating and retaining the *desire* and *exclusivity* attributions of luxury brands on the mass and the classless Internet while maintaining and enhancing the equity of the brand (Okonkwo 2009). Consumers in developing countries and emerging markets often have limited access to Internet technology. But the use of the Internet in Colombia has increased explosively and so can be used as a source of information and communications, making it an effective marketing tool for businesses. As such, Colombia has a strong media presence, which makes luxury brands very desirable. Not surprisingly, elites in urban areas in Latin America tend to exhibit the highest connectivity (Warf 2009). Elite consumers can travel abroad to buy luxury products, but the Internet provides a way to conquer distance. In addition, it helps them gather information beforehand and obtain products that are unavailable in local luxury stores—an instinct to own conspicuous luxury products (Zinkhan 2005). So, they can take advantaage of online shopping for luxury products.

Online shopping also leads consumers to time saving and better decision making. Oline shopping provides efficiency gains not only to consumers but also to retailers. Retailers save in selling time if consumers come in armed with information (Ratchford, Lee, & Talukdar 2003). Online marketing is able to target the needs of consumers directly by providing additional information such as comparisons, product reviews (though these can be fake!), what others bought, recent models, etc. Also, consumers are not under pressure to buy online, though some tactics can be used to apply pressure, such as stating that only one or two items are left, or that a promotion will end in a day, for example. Nowadays, online marketing uses artificial intelligence technology to target customers very precisely by identifying their search pattern and Internet Protocal (IP) addresses.

One of the issues in online marketing is that users determine page views depending upon where and how often they click on items within a session. This contrasts with traditional media in which the broadcaster/publisher controls the delivery of advertisements to its audience (Danaher 2007).

Global Orientation

Elite consumers are highly educated and well traveled and have a global orientation. The global orientation aspect of consumers seeks global luxury brands to satisfy their needs. The high value placed on foreign products and services is influenced by other people's perceptions, the availability, and the desire to fit in elite society. These consumers seek country-of-origin information that confirms the social status of a particular purchase and its popularity among their family and friends. Consumers may buy products made in certain countries to impress both family and peers (Khan, Bamber, & Quazi 2012). However, exceptions may exist with consumers who have very high nationalistic feelings and ethnocentric beliefs, and thus may have a negative attitude towards foreign products and services. But these feelings seem to diminish among customers with high global identity (Guo 2013). In the Colombian context, it does not seem to be applicable much, particularly in the case of luxury brands. Indeed, the growing materialistic values, new forms of social emulation, and increasing worldliness create demand for luxury products (Truong 2010).

Infrastructure

Colombia has underdeveloped infrastructure. Although Colombia has many seaports and rivers that increase its import and export abilities, the underdeveloped road system creates a burden on many businesses and trade agreements. The national road network remains a potential bottleneck, though it has improved in big cities. The Colombian government expects to invest in highway construction, tunnels, railroads, and ports, and also build Metro-Cable lines and *escalators* to connect isolated mountainside boroughs. Many branded products and services are unavailable in rural areas because of the poor infrastructure and the higher cost of doing business (Sheth 2011). Connecting boroughs to city centers would create more economic activities and availability of luxury brands in interior areas. From the retailers' viewpoint, it may still be challenging to keep luxury stores safe, arrange credit, and get people to and from stores. In many areas, the transportation infrastructure is weak or may be nonexistent. However, Colombia's various public-private partnerships are expected to contribute to development of the country and alleviate some of the issues relating to safety, security, and banking as well (Drummond, Dizgun, & Keeling 2012).

Note: This case study is designed to stimulate debate in the classroom by discussing issues relating to marketing and management of luxury and fashion products and services in the global business environment. It does not intend to illustrate the country's effectiveness or ineffectiveness in tackling the issues.

References

Atsmon, Y., Kuentz, J.F. & Seong, J. 2012. Building brands in emerging markets. *McKinsey Quarterly*, 4, 50–57.

Berthon, P., Pitt, L., Parent, M., & Berthon, J. 2009. Aesthetics and ephemerality: Observing and preserving the luxury brand. *California Management Review*, 52(1), 45–65.

Danaher, P.J. 2007. Modeling page views across multiple websites with an application to internet reach and frequency prediction. *Marketing Science*, 26(3), 422–437.

Drummond, H., Dizgun, J. & Keeling, D.I. 2012. Medellin: A city reborn? *American Geographical Society's Focus on Geography*, 55(4), 146–154.

Guo, X. 2013. Living in a global world: Influence of consumer global orientation on attitudes toward global brands from developed versus emerging countries. *Journal of International Marketing*, 21(1), 1–22.

Kaufmann, L. & Roesch, J. 2012. Constraints to building and deploying marketing capabilities by emerging market firms in advanced markets. *Journal of International Marketing*, 20(4), 1–24.

Khan, H., Bamber, D. & Quazi, A. 2012. Relevant or redundant: Elite consumers' perception of foreign-made products in an emerging market. *Journal of Marketing Management*, 28(9/10), 1190–1216.

Kumar, V., Sharma, A., Shah, R. & Rajan, B. 2013. Establishing profitable customer loyalty for multinational companies in the emerging economies: A conceptual framework. *Journal of International Marketing*, 21(1), 57–80.

Lee, R., Klobas, J., Tezinde, T. & Murphy, J. 2010. The underlying social identities of a nation's brand. *International Marketing Review*, 27(4), 450–465.

London, T. & Hart, S.L. 2004. Reinventing strategies for emerging markets: Beyond the transnational model. *Journal of International Business Studies*, 35(5), 350–370.

Okonkwo, U. 2009. Sustaining the luxury brand on the internet. *Brand Management*, 16(5), 302–310.

Ratchford, B.T., Lee, M. & Talukdar, D. 2003. The impact of the internet on information search for automobiles. *Journal of Marketing Research*, 40(2), 193–209.

Sheth, J.N. 2011. Impact of emerging markets on marketing: Rethinking existing perspectives and practices. *Journal of Marketing*, 75(4), 166–182.

Shukla, P. 2012. The influence of value perceptions on luxury purchase intentions in developed and emerging markets. *International Marketing Review*, 29(6), 574–596.

Truong, Y. 2010. Personal aspirations and the consumption of luxury goods. *International Journal of Market Research*, 52(5), 653–671.

Warf, B. 2009. Diverse specialities of the Latin American and Caribbean Internet. *Journal of Latin American Geography*, 8(2), 125–145.

Zinkhan, G.M. 2005. The marketplace, emerging technology and marketing theory. *Marketing Theory*, 5, 105–115.

10 Indonesia

Economy

Indonesia has undergone many changes in its political, economic, and social landscapes. The collapse of Indonesia's authoritarian government in 1998 led to the ushering in of a new era of democracy and economic growth. Growth in the Indonesian economy is mainly due to the increase in infrastructure support and development of human capital through education (Resosudarmo & Vidyattama 2006). This consistent growth and the establishment of a free market economy boosted demand for luxury products such as luxury cars, apartments, and real estate. Demand for prestigious and expensive cars—Ferrari and Maserati—particularly increased (McBeth 2003). Consumer spending, political stability, stable prices, and access to consumer credit fueled luxury consumption in Indonesia as well (ICM 2012). As a result, Indonesian markets are receptive to the appeal of luxury products. Although Indonesia has seen consistent and sustained economic growth with low unemployment of about 5 percent, it is estimated that more than half of employment in Indonesia is still in the informal sector. In rural areas, the informal economy constitutes more than 80 percent of employment (II 2020). The term *informal economy* means low and unstable income and reduced access to good amenities. Even those who manage to find consistent work in informal economies often find themselves in an employment situation that does not afford them the opportunity to advance themselves in life or to meet their own potential.

Wealth Disparity

Wealth disparity remains an issue in Indonesia. Wealth in Indonesia tends to be highly concentrated and geographically centralized. The inner provinces tend to hold much of the wealth, whereas the outer provinces have a higher tendency towards poverty (Schwarz 1997). For example, the GDP per capita in the inner provinces can be ten times that of the outer provinces. Variance in the provincial income per capita in Indonesia, as a result, is significantly higher than that of other emerging markets such as Mexico, the Philippines, and Pakistan (Resosudarmo & Vidyattama 2006). This high wealth disparity leads to a concentration of affluent consumers. These affluent customers are usually in inner urban areas where luxury products can be retailed. However, luxury brands are now able to reach rural communities and cities, which makes these brands more desirable and accessible to consumers in Indonesia (Bakht 2010). As such, Indonesia is vast, and the intricate chain of many islands naturally presents unique challenges for supply chain management. But Indonesia's improving retail infrastructure should boost the country's luxury sector (Gibson & Olivia 2010; Herabadi, Verplanken, & van Knippenberg 2009). Because of the conservative nature of the rural areas and the prevalence of Islamic (*Sharia*) laws, some luxury fashion brands may choose to be present in urban areas only.

Islamic Fashion

Islam plays a large role in women's choice of dress and fashion accessories. Islam provides a distinct set of consumption norms and the blueprint for its followers. Islamic consumption norms in Indonesia may not give the person much choice to pick what they want. For example, a woman may not be able to express herself with a necklace but must use a hijab instead. A Muslim woman may express a belief in Islam through a color of the hijab and the style of it (Coşgel & Minkler 2004). Religion accounts for differences in consumption habits of consumers in different areas of the world (Moschis & Ong 2011). But religion per se is not a critical factor in making clothing choices. Women in the *abaya* in Kuwait may be less about religious practices and more about expressing their cultural background. Even within Islamic religion, the style of cloth or the way it is worn can be different. For example, an *abaya* in Turkey can be very stylistic and modern (e.g. looking like a Western overcoat with a wide stylish collar and big buttons), whereas in Indonesia it may look overly long and conservative. It is also important to consider how ethnic dress is worn. In other Islamic nations such as in Kuwait, younger females wear the *abaya* on their shoulders and grasp it shut, whereas older females also hold it closed below the chin, but are more apt to wear it on their heads (Kelly 2010). Therefore, many Muslims may decide based on the region and what the religion inscribes about expressing identity. This is important in luxury marketing in Indonesia, because women may need different luxury products from Western women to satisfy the same needs. Even the stylistic differences may matter.

Halal Certification

Indonesia is home to the largest number of Muslims in the world. The religion greatly impacts the attitude and behavior of a Muslim, as Islam is a way of life. The religion prohibits and stipulates acceptable behaviors relating to consumption, a term called *halal*. Thus, Muslims are restricted in terms of consumption and purchase decisions. Halal also represents ritual cleanliness that follows the order of Allah (Ergul 2013). Halal encompasses a set of commandments implemented by Islam that Muslims must follow and comply with. Accordingly, businesses operating in Indonesia need to take special care to ensure their products are compliant with halal restrictions and rules. In this regard, halal labeling is becoming extremely popular in Indonesia, which ensures Indonesian halal-conscious consumers that their products are indeed halal-compliant (Luthfi & Salehudin 2011). Halal certification—a logo display—is commonly used by marketers and manufacturers to inform consumers that the products are halal-compliant (Shafie & Othman 2006). Halal integrity among consumers must be established and producers must agree on a benchmark for halal standards (Hashim & Ceo 2010). This requires collaboration from various governments, businesses, and Islamic organizations. Other than food, there are many halal-compliant luxury products such as halal cosmetics, nail polish, etc.

The Outlets

Indonesians usually buy luxury products from Hong Kong and Singapore. Singapore is particularly attractive to consumers as the same item costs less because of lower import duties. Another unique characteristic of luxury brands in Indonesia is the role of flagship stores. Indonesians love shopping at flagship stores, as it gives a feeling of shopping in a European country. Shopping malls prove to be the best way to engage consumers. Along with the increasing popularity of high-involvement products such as mobile phones and cars, spending on advertising in newspapers is also growing, as this medium provides a better space to demonstrate product features. Shopping malls, especially mega malls, have become a center for luxury products and lifestyle displays that provide opportunities to interact with a captive audience through in-mall traffic. The consumer pattern of shopping in mega malls is likely to continue to satisfy the increasingly sophisticated lifestyle needs resulting from the rise of middle-class income (Davis 2012).

Education

Indonesian consumers are relatively well educated. Indonesia has seen a consistent rise in education levels over a significant period of time. During 1967–2008, the rate of educational attainment increased an average of 3 percent every year. Using data collected during 1989–1999, it was found that the income of a person increases an average of 11 percent for every additional year of education they complete in Indonesia (Van der Eng 2010). This consistent increase in the level of educational attainment plays a particularly significant role in the marketing of luxury products. With the rise of the education level and disposable income of the middle class, the demand for luxury products and the desire to display status also increase. Middle-class consumers in Indonesia have turned towards luxury brands as their income has risen in recent years. The growing number of middle-class Indonesians has begun to spend more on both foreign and locally branded products.

The younger generations of Indonesians are delighted to spend money on big-ticket items that showcase wealth. Factors such as experience and self-reward have become part of the lifestyle among the wealthy (Davis 2011). As the number of well-off Indonesians increases, the level of sophistication and lifestyle aspirations is also expected to evolve. Shopping has become a major leisure and lifestyle activity for luxury products. Indeed, Indonesians like luxury, appreciate quality, and value craftsmanship (MAI 2007).

Note: This case study is designed to stimulate debate in the classroom by discussing issues relating to marketing and management of luxury and fashion products and services in the global business environment. It does not intend to illustrate the country's effectiveness or ineffectiveness in tackling the issues.

References

Bakht, A. 2010. Brands seek a place in the Indonesian country. *Media: Asia's Media & Marketing Newspaper*, 16.

Coşgel, M. & Minkler, L. 2004. Religious identity and consumption. *Review of Social Economy*, 62(3), 339–350.

Davis, C. 2011. Luxury report: A new frontier: Indonesia. *Campaign Asia-Pacific*, 3.

Davis, C. 2012. Indonesia report: Decoding the consumer. *Campaign Asia-Pacific*, 60.

Ergul, H.S. 2013. Religious industry in halal food consumption. *The Journal of Academic Social Science Studies*, 6(2), 831–841.

Gibson, J. & Olivia, S. 2010. The effect of infrastructure access and quality on non-farm enterprises in rural Indonesia. *World Development*, 38(5), 717–726.

Hashim, D.D. & Ceo, I.A. 2010. The quest for a global halal standard. In Meat Industry Association of New Zealand Annual Conference, Christchurch, 19–20.

Herabadi, A.G., Verplanken, B. & van Knippenberg, A. 2009. Consumption experience of impulse buying in Indonesia: Emotional arousal and hedonistic considerations. *Asian Journal of Social Psychology*, 12(1), 20–31.

ICM. 2012. Economic growth: Consumer demand, recent developments. *Indonesia Country Monitor (ICM)*, 6–7.

II. 2020. Indonesia investments. www.indonesia-investments.com/finance/macro economic-indicators/unemployment/item255 [Accessed on July 2, 2020].

Kelly, M. 2010. Clothes, culture, and context: Female dress in Kuwait. *Fashion Theory: The Journal of Dress, Body & Culture*, 14(2), 215–236.

Luthfi, B. & Salehudin, I. 2011. Marketing impact of halal labeling toward Indonesian Muslim consumer's behavioral intention based on Ajzen's planned behavior theory: Policy capturing studies on five different product categories. *ASEAN Marketing Journal*, 3(1), 33.

MAI. 2007. Macro-accessibility in Indonesia: Marketing Products and Services. *Indonesia Economic Studies*, 17–28.

McBeth, J. 2003. Indonesia's rich are back. *Far Eastern Economic Review*, 166(32), 44–45.

Moschis, G.P. & Ong, F.S. 2011. Religiosity and consumer behavior of older adults: A study of subcultural influences in Malaysia. *Journal of Consumer Behaviour*, 10(1), 8–17.

Resosudarmo, B. & Vidyattama, Y. 2006. Regional income disparity in Indonesia. *ASEAN Economic Bulletin*, 23(1), 31–44.

Schwarz, A. 1997. Indonesia after Suharto. *Foreign Affairs*, 76(4), 119–134.

Shafie, S. & Othman, M.N. 2006. Halal certification: An international marketing issues and challenges. In proceeding at the International IFSAM VIII World Congress, 28–30.

Van Der Eng, P. 2010. The sources of long-term economic growth in Indonesia, 1880–2008. *Explorations in Economic History*, 47, 294–309.

11 Vietnam

Luxury

Vietnam has a growing luxury consumer market as a result of its rising income, foreign direct investment, and liberalization of the economy. Vietnamese consumers are increasingly willing and able to spend on luxury products (Maruyama & Trung 2012). The tremendous growth in Vietnam in a short time has led to the creation of new wealth and an increase in disposable income, making it a promising market for both local and international businesses. Vietnam imported $10b worth of luxury products in 2010 (Ngo 2012). The luxury market is expected to experience a growth of 10 percent a year (Weidmann & Hennings 2013). Demand for luxury status–based products and services is high in Vietnam. Luxury brands such as Audi, Burberry, and Louis Vuitton appear to cater to the needs of Vietnam's emerging capitalist mentality very well. It is difficult to acquire an exact number of Vietnamese millionaires as they tend to keep their assets in cash (Genet 2008). Also, Vietnamese usually do not flaunt their wealth for cultural reasons. However, luxury is a status symbol for them. Western ideals are not rooted in Vietnamese culture, but it has seen the influence of American consumerism and the success of globalization. The luxury clothing and fashion industry is one of the fastest growing industries in Vietnam. The country is expanding its consumer purchasing ability, which attracts many global luxury brands and retailers. However, one of the limitations for luxury retailers in Vietnam is the lack of development of operational infrastructure because of political hurdles and excessive red tape (Collins 2008). This limits the ability of retailers and consumers to sell and buy luxury products, respectively.

Consumer Preferences

Country of origin (COO) plays an important role in luxury marketing in Vietnam. The COO decreases purchase likelihood when it is from an emerging market (Melnyk, Klein, & Völckner 2012). Vietnamese consumers tend to purchase products associated with America if they identify themselves as Vietnamese-Americans or have been socialized to believe American products are superior (Taylor, Babin, & Kim 2005). Vietnamese who are exposed to American culture are less likely to rely on others' behaviors and opinions for guidance in establishing shopping preferences.

More than 80 percent of Vietnamese people live in rural areas. The remaining 20 percent, who reside in urban areas, accounts for large expenditures on luxury products (Mai, Jung, Lantz, & Loeb 2003). This unequal income distribution gives rise to a disproportionately high demand for luxury products regardless of the economic climate, making Vietnam an ideal place to sell luxury goods. Further, disparities in living standards across ethnic groups also exist in Vietnam. The ethnic groups that experience the highest growth rate tend to have the highest living standards and therefore tend to be consumers of luxury goods (Baulch, Thi, Chuyen, Haughton, & Haughton 2002). Indeed, consumers' ethnic cultural identity and their product preferences are related.

Culture

Vietnam has one of the most complex ethno-linguistic patterns in Asia (Britannica 2020). *Culture* relates to way of life of people and everything one would need to know to become a functioning member of a society (Geertz 1973). In another definition of culture, it is about publicly available symbolic forms through which people experience and express meaning (Swidler 1986). Culture is also shaped by every aspect of a society such as history, socio-economic and political ideologies, and military successes and failures, among others. In the context of Vietnam, its culture can be considered as collectivistic as it values family, positive reputations, love of learning, and respect for other people (Mai, Jung, Lantz, & Loeb 2003). Old generations of pre-economic reform still exhibit characteristics of collectivistic culture and are tied to the Vietnamese tradition. However, over the years, the culture has shifted towards individualistic because of economic transformation and the young generations' exposure to globalization. Collectivistic cultures are less likely to indulge in impulse buying as opposed to individualistic cultures (Kacen & Lee 2002).

Consumer Behavior

The majority of Vietnamese consumers are between the ages of 18 and 35, so they have experienced Western culture and consumerism. It is difficult for the segment to stay within the traditional cultural boundaries of Vietnam. The rapidly growing middle class and a dominant youthful population have resulted in a significant increase in the demand for status-generating products such as luxury cars, jewelry, clothing, and electronics, among others. The emerging individualistic nature of the society also has impact on impulse buying behavior, as buyers can make decisions individually rather than engaging in actions most beneficial to their family and community. In the past, Vietnamese consumers did not have access to luxury products as much, and therefore they would repair the item to extend its life. Now, the ready availability of luxury products in stores or online encourages luxury purchases, whether planned or impulsive. In fact, impulse buying behavior in Vietnam appears to match that in Western societies; however, impulse buying is not as extravagant in nature, as Vietnamese consumers look for value in their purchases, even though they are focused on purchasing status-enhancing products. They prefer value to excessive pricing. So luxury brands need to convince Vietnamese consumers that the value created is worth more than its price tag (Speece & Nair 2000). Indeed, these products are likely to have potential for positive self-presentation, self-expression, and mood adjustment (Kacen & Lee 2002). These products are often expensive. Vietnam is increasingly becoming more materialistic because of the globalization of primarily Western values. Vietnam is a youthful country for marketing fashion, at least.

Note: This case study is designed to stimulate debate in the classroom by discussing issues relating to marketing and management of luxury and fashion products and services in the global business environment. It does not intend to illustrate the country's effectiveness or ineffectiveness in tackling the issues.

References

Baulch, B., Thi, T., Chuyen, K., Haughton, D. & Haughton, J. 2002. Ethnic minority development in Vietnam: A socioeconomic perspective. World Bank Policy Research Working Paper 2836, 1–18.

Britannica. 2020. www.britannica.com [Accessed on July 2, 2020].

Collins, P. 2008. Half-way from rags to riches: A special report on Vietnam. *Economist Newspaper*, April 28.

Geertz, C. 1973. Thick description: Toward an interpretive theory of culture. *Critical Concepts in Sociology*, 1, 173–196.

Genet, A. 2008. In Vietnam, new money fuels boom in luxury goods. www.thingsasian. com/stories-photos/30431 [Accessed on July 2, 2020].

Kacen, J.J. & Lee, J.A. 2002. The influence of culture on consumer impulsive buying behavior. *Journal of Consumer Psychology*, 12(2), 163–176.

Mai, N.T.T., Jung, K., Lantz, G. & Loeb, S.G. 2003. An exploratory investigation into impulse buying behavior in a transitional economy: A study of urban consumers in Vietnam. *Journal of International Marketing*, 11(2), 13–35.

Maruyama, M. & Trung, L. 2012. Modern retailers in transition economies: The Case of Vietnam. *Journal of Macromarketing*, 32(1), 31–51.

Melnyk, V., Klein, K. & Völckner, F. 2012. The double-edged sword of foreign brand names for companies from emerging countries. *Journal of Marketing*, 76(6), 21–37.

Ngo, T.V. 2012. Vietnam 90 Million Consumers. *Intereffekt Investment Funds*, 1–3.

Speece, M. & Nair, G. 2000. Value oriented shopping behavior amongst urban middle class Vietnamese consumers. *Asian Academy of Management Journal*, 5(1), 45–54.

Swidler, A. 1986. Culture in action: Symbols and strategies. *American Sociological Review*, 51(2), 273–286.

Taylor, C.R., Babin, B.J. & Kim, K.H. 2005. Marketing to Asian Americans: The impact of acculturation and interpersonal influence on ethnocentric consumer preferences. *Journal of Global Academy of Marketing Science*, 15(3), 187–210.

Weidmann, K.P. & Hennings, N. 2013. *Luxury marketing: A challenge for theory and practice*. Gabler Verlag: Hannover.

12 South Africa

The Segment

South Africa is among the most unequal societies in the world (McDonald & Piesse 1999). Although there is significant inequity in wealth distribution, where many in the population still consider furniture, transportation, clothing, and recreation as luxuries, the number of wealthy citizens is growing rapidly (Selvanathan & Selvanathan 2004). One of the factors that has contributed to the emergence of this wealthy class is the new policy—Black Economic Empowerment—that seeks to offer economic opportunities to the previously disadvantaged in a society characterized by *apartheid*. The policy has propelled people from living in poverty to affluence. It is a very visible new type of luxury consumer, known to retailers as *Black Diamonds* (Mpehle 2011). It has been reported that there were only about 638,000 affluent individuals with more than $50k in liquid assets in 2010. However, with the prospect of growth, the number of individuals with an asset band of $1m to $1.5m is scheduled to increase significantly (Botegga 2011). The number of millionaires in Africa rose about 4 percent in 2012, which is a faster growth than any other region, except for South America (Sulaiman 2012). Indeed, South Africa is now producing millionaires at an astonishing rate, resulting in an environment conducive to luxury marketing.

Tourism

Tourism is a major component of the luxury market in South Africa. The country has been able to compete in the luxury market by creating a luxury tourism market. This is a rapidly growing area of tourism that brings affluent tourists from across the globe. Many tour operators offer luxury services to tourists and contribute to local economies. Some luxury tours offer more than 60 resorts, exotic food, safari camps, and self-driven adventures. Tours such as these are becoming very popular in catering to the wealthy. Luxury tour operators compete against one another on their ability to evoke rarity and exclusivity. The rarity aspect is particularly important in the South African tourism industry because the country is home to rare animals and deserts, making safaris an important tourist draw. Indeed, the rarity principle affects the consumption of luxury tourism. In the post-apartheid environment, South Africa has emerged as a leader and innovator in strategic planning and promotion of domestic tourism to cities and towns (Rogerson & Visser 2007).

In another case, South Africa offers wine tourism as a niche market (Du Rand, Heath, & Alberts 2003). The Stellenbosch district in South Africa is most known for its wine production and tourism. This area has evolved over the years. Some resorts offer the best in luxury wine tourism, attracting wine connoisseurs from within South Africa and around the globe. These resorts offer wine-tasting centers, major restaurants, coffee shops with gardens, 18-hole golf courses, assorted entertainment venues, a railway station to bring in people, nature experience complexes, large sports complexes, four- and five-star hotels, and much more (Demhardt 2003).

Gay tourism is also popular in South Africa. Cape Town has emerged as the *gay capital* of Africa. Over the years, De Waterkant has developed into a place for wealthy, white gay males and has become prosperous as a result of catering to the wealthy gay community. Cape Town markets itself globally as a gay-friendly place by offering special events and showcasing the De Waterkant area's gay businesses, bringing in mostly wealthier gay men from around the world (Visser 2003). Positioning of the gay-friendly city has additional benefits to tourism in that it shows that South Africa is open to others' beliefs, and is thus an inclusive society and country. The gay community, with its generally higher wealth, is more likely to be customers of luxury products and services as well.

Houses

South Africa is a second-home country to many rich people. Luxury houses are high-equity growth products. Wealthy people in South Africa buy second homes outside of their metropolitan areas. For example, Greyton used to be a small agricultural town but now is reserved strictly for the wealthy. Accordingly, tourism and hospitality industries in these areas have grown because upper-income people reside here seasonally (Donaldson 2009). In fact, the total average amount that second-home owners and renters spend on restaurants, art galleries, and gas, among other commodities, is exorbitant and viewed as luxury in nature (Hoogendoorn & Visser 2010). South African tourism competes in the global marketplace and benefits from the global demand for second homes (Cornelissen 2005). Another luxury tourist attraction for this segment is golfing and hunting (Keenan 2007).

Political Ideology and Fashion

Fashion acts as a communication tool for individuals to demonstrate their political identity and ideology. The political ideology of a nation affects the lives of its citizens. Consumers use fashion discourses to forge self-defining social distinctions and boundaries, to construct narratives of personal history, and to interpret social spheres (Thompson & Haytko 1997). A political ideology is a theory of reality that motivates the ordering of reality into good and bad, right and wrong, and them and us and provides the members of society with the basic tenets of mentality about and how life ought to be lived (Eagleton 1991; Mikkonen, Vicdan, & Markkula 2001). The tension between ethnic fashion and colonial Western fashion in South Africa is striking. The country has undergone immense changes and passed through colonial history, formalized apartheid, and witnessed its official demise. Reformative changes have brought South African culture and society into post-colonial cultural, racial, and political identities that are being reframed on different political and psychological terms (Levin 2005). Ethnic fashion was used as a tool to resist colonial rule in South Africa. Fashion also portrays power differences. Colonial powers influenced ethnic dress in South Africa. Ethnic and colonial fashion designers have been collaborating profoundly in South African society to act as a bridge to repair previous racial conflicts. Ethnic fashion is politically significant, because it is an indicator of group identity and a means of developing and strengthening ethnic, religious, or political solidarity (Hopkin 2006). Fashion has provided a medium for ameliorating the historical inequalities of apartheid and has been a part of the reconstruction of South African identity post-1994 (Farber 2010). South Africa's ethnic fashion therefore is endowed with political significance and importance. It represents more than mere individual preference. Ethnic fashion in South Africa represents the struggle to retain historic cultural values amid a colonial power. By expressing these statements, consumers distinguish themselves from alternate values and meanings. In this way, symbolic consumption has become associated with identity politics (Murray 2002). Ideology influences consumers of fashion. Therefore, fashion and ethnic fashion products are much more complex, as they carry political and ideological significance.

Infrastructure

The lack of retail space in South Africa is an issue for luxury retailers. If there were more retail space in South Africa, such as malls, more luxury investors could be attracted (Sulaiman 2012). Infrastructure is an important factor in market expansion. Although the lack of secured retail space is currently a hurdle for South Africa to expanding its luxury market, it could be overcome with proper investment.

Note: This case study is designed to stimulate debate in the classroom by discussing issues relating to marketing and management of luxury and fashion products and services in the global business environment. It does not intend to illustrate the country's effectiveness or ineffectiveness in tackling the issues.

References

Botegga, S. 2011. *Market snapshot: South Africa*. Johannesburg: Southern Africa Luxury Association.

Cornelissen, S. 2005. Producing and imaging 'place' and 'people': The political economy of South African international tourist representation. *Review of International Political Economy*, 12(4), 674–699.

Demhardt, I.J. 2003. Wine and tourism at the *fairest cape*: Post-apartheid trends in the western Cape province and Stellenbosch. *Journal of Travel & Tourism Marketing*, 14(3), 113–130.

Donaldson, R. 2009. The making of a tourism-gentrified town: Greyton, South Africa. *Geography*, 94(2), 88.

du Rand, G., Heath, E. & Alberts, N. 2003. The role of local and regional food in destination marketing: A South African situation analysis. *Journal of Travel & Tourism Marketing*, 14(3), 97–112.

Eagleton, T. 1991. *Ideology: An introduction*. London: Verso. 1–2.

Farber, L. 2010. Africanising hybridity? Toward an Afropolitan aesthetic in contemporary South African fashion design. *Critical Arts*, 24(1), 128–167.

Hoogendoorn, G. & Visser, G. 2010. The role of second homes in local economic development in five small South African towns. *Development Southern Africa*, 27(4), 547–562.

Hopkin, M. 2006. *Fashioning Africa: Power and the politics of dress*. Bloomington: Indiana University Press.

Keenan, T. 2007. Targeting the tourists. *Finweek*, 28–32.

Levin, A. 2005. Seshoeshoe chic hits the streets: Styles of the times. *Fairlady*, 74–79.

McDonald, S. & Piesse, J. 1999. Legacies of apartheid: The distribution of income in South Africa. *Journal of International Development*, 11(7), 985–1004.

Mikkonen, I., Vicdan, H. & Markkula, A. 2001. What not to wear? Oppositional ideology, fashion, and governmentality in wardrobe self-help. *Consumption Markets and Culture*, 17(3), 255–256.

Mpehle, Z. 2011. Black economic empowerment. *Association of Southern African Schools and Departments of Public Administration and Management*, 19(3).

Murray, J.B. 2002. Re-inquiries—the politics of consumption: A re-inquiry on Thompson and Haytko's 1997 'speaking of fashion'. *The Journal of Consumer Research*, 29(3), 427.

Rogerson, C.M. & Visser, G. 2007. *Urban tourism in the developing world: The South African experience*. New Brunswick: Transaction.

Selvanathan, S. & Selvanathan, E.A. 2004. Empirical regularities in South African consumption patterns. *Applied Economics*, 36(20), 2327–2333.

Sulaiman, T. 2012. Luxury industry's next frontier: Africa. *The Globe & Mail*.

Thompson, C.J. & Haytko, D.L. 1997. Speaking of fashion: Consumers' uses of fashion discourses and the appropriation of countervailing cultural meanings. *Journal of Consumer Research*, 24(1), 15–42.

Visser, G. 2003. Gay men, tourism and urban space: Reflections on Africa's 'gay capital'. *Tourism Geographies*, 5(2), 1.

Part IV
Cases on Luxury Brands

13 Apple

Apple products are unique and fast and have incredible feather-touch capabilities. Product operations are intuitive, straightforward, and easy to use. Apple products are sturdy, look attractive, and are made from astounding materials, with micro precision in mind. Apple led the digital music revolution with its iPods and iTunes online store. Apple reinvented the mobile phone with its revolutionary iPhone and App store and redefined the future of mobile media, marketing, and computing devices. Apple iPhones are one of the most popular smartphones worldwide. The phones have been able to automatically update apps since iOS7. Apple's aspiration for thinner and lighter designs and convenience makes it an essential and unique product. As a result, Apple products have a great reputation; they are sleek, have a modern design, and are desirable. Their popularity and high price tag make them luxury products. Apple products have their own personality, which gives them a distinct look and creativity. Even the logo looks clean and attractive. In short, people love Apple products.

Apple's first logo was designed by Ronald Wayne. It was large, detailed, and black and white, depicting Newton sitting under a tree. Apple Computer Co. was also written on the logo. Then the logo changed to become simpler, with a rainbow color spectrum. Because the Apple logo was recognizable by then, there was no need to state the company's name. However, CEO Steve Jobs still wanted something simpler and modern. The logo was then upgraded to what we see now—a subtle and contemporary logo.

Although Apple is a desirable product, it is not without controversy. A major issue relates to the *battery degrading solution*—that is, the slowing or possibly shutting down of old iPhones with the release of new iPhones. Apple customers saw the timing and solution as a promotion trick to encourage them to purchase the latest-model devices. Apple admitted to slowing down older models to compensate for the battery degradation process, after multiple accusations from consumers. This resulted in older iPhone users losing trust in Apple, because the company failed to inform them of their plan to modify their devices in iOS updates and provide inadequate information about their aging batteries.

More recently, Apple faced consumer wrath for removing screen time and parental control apps from its store. Removing parental controls made it difficult for parents to monitor their children's activities on the Internet. The removal favored those who were addicted to iPhones or similar tools. Apple's reasoning for removing the apps was that developers were using mobile device management (MDM) and virtual personal networks (VPNs) in parental control apps to obtain information such as location, app use, email accounts, camera permission, and browsing history. Hackers could also use the MDM and VPN technologies. MDM enables parents to take control of a child's phone, whereas VPN blocks certain apps on a child's iPhone. However, Apple backtracked later and introduced a more secured version of the control app. Although the issue is resolved for now, it is a reminder of the power Apple wields over its store as to who is allowed to sell there or not.

In the context of the emerging market in India, Apple faced significant hurdles to making inroads with sales. Apple products proved to be too expensive compared with other available brands that cost a third of what Apple charges. Apple is expensive in India, because it does not have manufacturing facilities there as do other competitors. Therefore, Apple needs to import products to India and pay a high import duty to do so, although it does make low-value items in India. Also, the dilemma for Apple is that new iPhones are too expensive but old or refurbished iPhones do not appeal to Indian customers, because the business practice may be seen as e-dumping. Or, customers' inability to afford new iPhones may put them at risk of being labeled as poor.

Another challenge for Apple is the distribution network in India. Corporate-owned mono brand stores need to source 30 percent of their goods locally (ANI 2016). However, this requirement can be waived by the Indian government for companies with cutting-edge technologies. Similar distribution issues exist for Apple products in Singapore. While true that the Apple brand is desirable, it has negatives as well. It needs to be managed and balanced with delicate business practices.

Note: This case study is designed to stimulate debate in the classroom by discussing issues relating to marketing and management of luxury and fashion products and services in the global business environment. It does not intend to illustrate the management's effectiveness or ineffectiveness in tackling the issues.

Reference

ANI. 2016. Apple fails to get 30 percent local sourcing waiver to open stores in India. www.financialexpress.com/industry/technology/apple-fails-to-get-30-per-cent-local-sourcing-waiver-to-open-stores-in-india [Accessed on July 6, 2020].

14 BMW

BMW (Bayerische Motoren Werke) was founded in 1916 (then Rapp Motorenwerke) to manufacture aircraft engines for the German air force during World War I. Following the war, it switched to making farm equipment and railway brakes. During the war, BMW facilities were bombed and damaged. The remaining facilities were banned from making motorcycles or automobiles. So, during the ban, they made items such as pens, kitchen supplies, and bicycles. After World War II, BMW was in debt, as luxury sedans did not sell enough to generate profit, and sales of motorcycles were greatly reduced. However, in 1962 the newly designed sedan proved to be very successful.

BMW's mission is to become the world's leading provider of premium products and services for individual mobility. Its slogan is: *Ultimate Driving Machine.*

The BMW logo is simple. It comprises white and blue quadrants that are enclosed within a circle. The black ring around the circle reads "BMW," with the letters spaced out across the top. The quadrants in combination look like a spinning aircraft propeller. No wonder; BMW used to make aircraft engines based on turbine technology. However, the choice of color for the logo is intriguing; the blue and white actually represent the Bavarian flag. Because BMW was not allowed to feature national coats of arms or other symbols of national sovereignty on their logo, they used the blue and white colors in the opposite order of the flag to ensure compliance with the German Act. It is one of the most recognizable luxury car logos.

BMW is known for its speed and performance. So, its engine needs to produce massive power to exert thrust, which also produces very high carbon emissions. BMW continually experiments to reduce its carbon footprint while enhancing engine performance. In the process of reducing carbon emissions, BMW drew controversy over its joint experiment with Volkswagen and Daimler, using caged monkeys that were forced to inhale diesel fumes for hours (Behrmann 2018; Kottasova 2018). The objective of the experiment was to prove that the newer engines were cleaner. During the experiment, the monkeys were shown cartoons to watch to keep them calm. Among European countries, Germany has one of the strictest animal testing laws, almost equivalent to banning all testing on apes as laboratory animals. Even in the US, this type of testing is not illegal, but these actions made animal rights advocates angry and upset. The controversy even drew the attention of German Chancellor Angela Merkel whose spokesman, Steffen Seibert, said, "These tests . . . are in no ethical way justifiable and they raise many critical questions about those who are behind the tests." Related to the experiment, it was also revealed that the vehicle used for the experiment was rigged to cheat diesel emissions (Ewing 2018). This was accomplished through emission-changing software that could sense when it was being tested. When on the roads, these cars could release up to 40 times the allowable levels of pollutants. Results of the experiment were not published on grounds that the experiment's conditions were compromised.

Note: This case study is designed to stimulate debate in the classroom by discussing issues relating to marketing and management of luxury and fashion products and services in the global business environment. It does not intend to illustrate the management's effectiveness or ineffectiveness in tackling the issues.

References

Behrmann, E. 2018. Volkswagen apologizes for testing of Diesel fumes on monkeys. www.bloomberg.com/news/articles/2018-01-28/volkswagen-apologizes-for-testing-of-diesel-fumes-on-monkeys [Accessed on July 6, 2020].

Ewing, J. 2018. BMW offices raided by authorities in emissions-cheating investigation. www.nytimes.com/2018/03/20/business/energy-environment/bmw-diesel-emissions.html [Accessed on July 6, 2020].

Kottasova, I. 2018. Volkswagen, BMW and Daimler research institute used monkeys to test diesel fumes, www.money.cnn.com/2018/01/29/investing/volkswagen-daimler-bmw-monkey-testing-diesel/index.html [Accessed on July 6, 2020].

15 Burberry

Burberry was founded in 1856. It became a leading global luxury fashion brand because of its invention of gabardine, patented trench coats, and the eponymous check pattern. Burberry is an elegant and classic brand whose motto is *Prorsum*, that is, "forward." The motto contributed to advancing the firm technologically to new heights. Its mission is to maintain integrity and vitality of the brand while remaining relevant to ever-evolving markets and consumer tastes (Burberry 2020).

The *Equestrian Knight* logo of Burberry is one of the most iconic insignias in fashion. The logo is clean, elegant, and detailed, and free from designs, flourishes, or punctuations. Historically, the logo was appropriate to represent the trench coat's utilitarian nature. However, a new visual identity was created in 2018 in which the knight was removed from the official logo, though it still appears on tags and packaging of the brand (Ferrier 2020a). The new logo reads simply "BURBERRY." The current logo is not big and bold, but subtle enough to stand out at the same time.

Burberry has embraced digital marketing techniques to render unique shopping experiences online or in physical stores, a very different strategy from other luxury brands that are ambivalent towards online marketing. So, Burberry aims to be accessible globally to markets and ship its products to its customers while producing the products in limited quantities and distributing them at luxury prices. In its desire to maintain exclusivity, Burberry ran into controversy when it burnt its overstock items, drawing the wrath of environmental activist groups. The reason for the destruction was to prevent the products from being sold on black or gray markets at reduced prices, thus devaluing the exclusive nature of the products (Ferrier 2020b). Burberry destroys about $20–30m of unsold products a year. However, Burberry has announced that it will try to reuse and revalue unsold products as much as possible (Paton 2018).

Burberry is also criticized for its use of genuine fur from rabbit, fox, mink, and Asiatic raccoon. Supporters of animal rights and animal abuse such as People for the Ethical Treatment of Animals (PETA) and London Fashion Week have voiced concern for fur-based products. But as of November 2017, other luxury brands—Louis Vuitton, Dior, Karl Lagerfeld, Yves Saint Laurent, Marc Jacob, and Fendi—were not fur free either. Some customers may find fur-based products unethical too. Although using real fur harms the animals, faux fur does not help the environment either, because it is made from petroleum-based plastic materials that are neither sustainable nor representative of luxury (Williamson 2018). In 2018, Burberry announced that it would put an end to burning its unsold goods and also stop selling products using natural fur. Burberry joins the ranks of major fashion brands—Armani, Versace, Gucci, Ralph Lauren, Vivienne Westwood, and Stella McCartney—that do not use natural fur (McDonald 2018). Burberry is now eager to introduce a new kind of luxury—modern luxury that is socially and environmentally responsible (Wood & Kollewe 2017). Burberry's decision has been hailed as cause for celebration by animal rights organizations. But the International Fur Federation remains disappointed, as faux fur is not environmentally friendly. Perhaps another alternative is needed for modern luxury?

Note: This case study is designed to stimulate debate in the classroom by discussing issues relating to marketing and management of luxury and fashion products and services in the global business environment. It does not intend to illustrate the management's effectiveness or ineffectiveness in tackling the issues.

References

Burberry. 2020. Our history, Burberry. https://ca.burberry.com/our-history [Accessed on July 6, 2020].

Ferrier, M. 2020a. Graphic artist Peter Saville on creating Burberry's new logo. www.theguardian.com/fashion/2019/feb/14/graphic-artist-peter-saville-on-creating-burberrys-new-logo [Accessed on July 6, 2020].

Ferrier, M. 2020b. Why does Burberry destroy its products and how is it justified? www.theguardian.com/fashion/2018/jul/20/why-does-burberry-destroy-its-products-q-and-a [Accessed on July 6, 2020].

McDonald, S. 2018. 9 Luxury brands that have stopped using fur in 2018. www.footwearnews.com/2018/fashion/designers/fur-free-luxury-fashion-brands-1202671394 [Accessed on July 6, 2020].

Paton, E. 2018. Burberry to stop burning clothing and other goods it can't sell. www.nytimes.com/2018/09/06/business/burberry-burning-unsold-stock.html [Accessed on July 6, 2020].

Williamson, H. 2018. Burberry has finally ditched fur—but faux fur has its own problems too. https://metro.co.uk/2018/09/07/burberry-has-finally-ditched-fur-but-faux-fur-has-its-own-problems-too-7919459 [Accessed on July 6, 2020].

Wood, Z. & Kollewe, J. 2017. Burberry to reinvent itself as a super luxury British brand. www.theguardian.com/business/2017/nov/09/burberry-to-reinvent-itself-as-a-super-luxury-british-brand [Accessed on July 6, 2020].

16 Gucci

Gucci was founded in Florence, Italy, in 1921. Gucci is innovative and timeless. It showcases its best craftsmanship and creativity in its products. Gucci is a brand whose designs are permanently stylish and recognizable. It is a powerful luxury brand with a global appeal. Gucci's mission is to become the leader of the luxury market worldwide. It is one of the world's most beloved luxury brands and instantly recognizable not only by its logo, but also by its Italian roots and quality.

Gucci's logo, with its double facing "Gs," has a bold and sophisticated look. Its striking, plain black style represents its excellence and dominance in fashion. The logo can also be seen in gold on more luxurious and extravagant products. The logo size varies depending on the nature of the product; for example, a large logo may ensure visibility on clothing, whereas a small logo may be appropriate on handbags. The interlocked pattern represents endlessness and dynamic nature. The logo is also supposed to signify its never-ending determination to reach new horizons and its devotion to the business. Gucci's dominance in the fashion industry with its excellence and integrity is remarkable.

Gucci defines high-end luxury through its quality products. But some issues and events have caused customers to turn away from the brand. At times designers are so keen on developing creativity and conveying messages that backlash from customers and critics occurs. Gucci's blackface balaclava sweatshirt and the Balmain Noose hoodie were not well received by consumers, particularly as the products were released during Black History Month. The shirt resembles *blackface* and makes fun of African Americans in the 1900s in the US (Ocbazghi & Skvaril 2019). However, Gucci states that it never intended to create something so sinister and racist (Griffth 2019). Gucci said that racism was not the intention behind the balaclava sweater—which featured a pull-up neck and bright red lips as a cut-out for the mouth. Gucci added, "We are coming from a different culture, we are Italian. We don't know the culture differences." This ill-conceived product design had a significant negative impact on the sales of Gucci and on the brand image. Celebrities were seen burning their Gucci shirts on social media platforms.

Following the outcry, Gucci removed the sweater from its stores and website after social media users denounced it as resembling blackface. Gucci deeply apologized for the offense caused by the wool balaclava jumper and said:

> We consider diversity to be a fundamental value to be fully upheld, respected, and at the forefront of every decision we make. We are fully committed to increasing the diversity throughout our organization and turning this incident into a powerful learning moment for the Gucci team and beyond.
>
> (Chiu 2019)

For a global brand, it is important to understand, appreciate, and respect local cultures and traditions worldwide. Indeed, it can be challenging given the spectrum of diversity and ethnicity worldwide, but information technology can offer some consolations.

Note: This case study is designed to stimulate debate in the classroom by discussing issues relating to marketing and management of luxury and fashion products and services in the global business environment. It does not intend to illustrate the management's effectiveness or ineffectiveness in tackling the issues.

References

Chiu, A. 2019. Haute couture blackface Gucci apologizes and pulls *racist* sweater. www.washingtonpost.com/nation/2019/02/07/haute-couture-blackface-gucci-apologizes-pulls-racist-sweater [Accessed on July 6, 2020].

Griffth, J. 2019. Gucci creative director says unintended racist imagery 890 sweater causes him grief. www.nbcnews.com/news/us-news/gucci-creative-director-says-unintended-racist-imagery-890-sweater-causes-n971261 [Accessed on July 6, 2020].

Ocbazghi, E. & Skvaril, C. 2019. Why these Gucci clothe are racist. www.businessinsider.com/why-gucci-clothes-racist-blackface-sambo-2019-2 [Accessed on July 6, 2020].

17 Conclusion

The purpose of the book was to provide innovative concepts that could be applicable in the marketing of luxury and fashion products and services in the context of the global environment. The chapter relating to mission statements finds that business managers can use clearly developed mission and vision statements to communicate their strategy and motivate their teams to achieve an inspiring common vision of the future. Although luxury brands typically tend to be associated with money, status, and quality, customers may also buy luxury products based on their perceptions of the brands, and the values and messages they convey to their stakeholders—internal or external—through the mission statements.

Logos are similar to mission statements in terms of conveying messages. The logo-based chapter indicates that the notion behind a successful and effective logo is to develop consumer recognition and recall of the company's brand. By creating a memorable image, a company is able to establish a lasting impression in the minds of their current and potential customers. Companies do this by creating innovative logos and by attaching a message about what the company's brand stands for. The influence of innovation and creativity in logo design stimulates customers' ability to recognize and identify a certain brand and its message. The more opportunities customers have to recognize a brand, the more they will depend on the brand to satisfy their needs.

Airports provide excellent opportunities for retailers to introduce their products to customers from around the world who have different demographics and psychographics. The airport retailing chapter describes how travelers usually feel relaxed after security checks and are willing to spend time browsing stores and thus are likely to engage in shopping behavior. However, airport retailers need to pay particular attention to apathetic shoppers, who are least interested in browsing, shopping, or conforming to impulse buying.

The marketing-related chapter discusses contemporary marketing tools in five areas: virtual reality; online marketing; social media (i.e. cost effectiveness, trust, status, brand equity, and visual capability); mobile marketing (i.e. smartphone, brand extension, and challenges); and celebrity endorsement (i.e. endorsement effects, celebrity reputation, and no endorsement strategy). Semiotic communications was also discussed for creating meaning for luxury brands through logos.

The chapter on luxury marketing discusses how luxury brands face challenges in marketing or engaging in publicity because of the very nature of luxury products and services—that is, being exclusive, subdued, and silent. The areas of the challenges were charity activities (e.g. cultural events, corporate philanthropy, community development, luxury shame, and controversies); counterfeit luxury products (e.g. who buys counterfeit products, the emerging market perspective, counterfeit luxury products life cycle, and counterfeit prevention); corporate social responsibility (e.g. sustainability and ethics); and government advertisement regulations.

In the context of fashion marketing, the next chapter explores political fashion, eco fashion, ethnic fashion, beachwear, and underwear fashion. Political fashion relates to someone who uses fashion to make a political statement. Eco fashion relates to the environment, whereas ethnic fashion covers gender and education and its impact on ethnic fashion. The chapter also discusses the marketing of luxury beachwear and underwear, and the impact of seasonality, age, and post-feminism on customer preferences and demand for such luxury undergarments. Another chapter relating to Indian fashion, which is influenced by Western luxury fashion brands as well, focuses on economy, culture, media, and films; the decision-making process; and marketing strategy.

Chapters 9, 10, 11, and 12 relate to case studies involving Colombia, Indonesia, Vietnam, and South Africa, respectively, whereas Chapters 13, 14, 15, and 16 relate to case studies on Apple, BMW, Burberry, and Gucci, respectively. These mini cases were selected carefully to generate discussion through the application of the concepts presented in this book.

Index

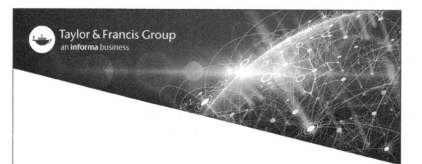

Printed in the United States
by Baker & Taylor Publisher Services